FINDING GOD IN THE FAST LANE

as well as in life's lay-bys

Joyce Huggett

eagle

Guildford, Surrey

British Library Cataloguing-in-Publication Data. A catalogue record for this book is available from the British Library.

Published by Eagle, an imprint of Inter Publishing Service (IPS) Ltd, 59 Woodbridge Road, Guildford, Surrey GU1 4RF.

All Scripture quotations, unless otherwise noted, are taken from the *Holy Bible, New International Version*. Copyright © 1973, 1978, 1984 by the International Bible Society. Used by permission of Hodder & Stoughton.

Photographic Credits
Front Cover © Robert Matheson, Zefa Picture Library UK Ltd.
Pages 16, 17 Acrylic, Martha and Mary, © Gael O'Leary RSM.
Pages 24, 45, 52, 73, 96, 100, 108, 120 © Len Smith, Lens Ideas
Pages 41, 65, 84, 113 © David Huggett
All photographs used with kind permission.

Typeset by The Electronic Book Factory, Fife, Scotland.
Printed in India

ISBN No: 0 86347 103X

CONTENTS

for
John and Jane
whose busy lives radiate Christ

ACKNOWLEDGEMENTS

As always, many people have supported me while I have been writing this book. Here there is space to mention only a few.

First, I would like to thank Kathleen Robinson and Meili Hawthorne, not only for inviting me to speak to the Women's Fellowship at St Nicholas' Church, Nottingham on the subject of 'The Practice of the Presence of God' but for their enthusiastic response to my talk which prompted me to consider writing up the material in book form.

Next, I owe a debt of gratitude to Deirdre Offord and Jacqui Swaine who also persuaded me that there is a pressing need for a book like *Finding God in the Fast Lane*.

Third, my thanks go to Sir John Ford for his warm response to the Bible Reading Fellowship notes I wrote on 'The Practice of the Presence of God' and for kindly granting me permission to quote from his own reflections on Brother Lawrence's book.

I would also like to express my thanks to the three people who have provided the photographs to illustrate the text: Gael O'Leary RSM (whom I mention again in the Introduction), my husband, David, whose pictures capture many happy memories for us both and Len Smith who read the text several times, travelled to Cyprus to take pictures of the area where I now live and who even went as far as meeting me while I was in transit at Heathrow Airport to show me the photographs he had taken.

My final vote of thanks goes to David Wavre, the Managing Director of Eagle. Working with an author living and working overseas is not easy – especially when that author is frequently unable to be contacted by telephone or fax. I am grateful for David's patience, encouragement and ongoing practical support – like taking me to and meeting me from airports at most unsociable hours and delaying publication to enable me to meet my deadlines.

Those who have prayerfully undergirded the gestation and birthing of this book will neither expect nor desire to be thanked. Even so, I would like to put on record that I am aware that I shall never be able to repay them. As I reflect on their commitment, I feel rich to have the support of so many faithful, praying people.

Joyce Huggett

INTRODUCTION

The realisation that we can encounter God anywhere and everywhere, even in the fast lane, first
excited me some thirty years ago. I was attending a
women's coffee morning in a hotel in Bournemouth
at the time.

The speaker was a friend of mine whom I had met
a few years earlier when I was a student. She was one
of those unforgettable people who exuded serenity
and peace, kindness and gentleness, calmness and
quietness – qualities which seemed to overflow from
her to fill every nook and cranny of her home and
garden. Yet she lived life to the full: enjoying her
family, friends and fun, supporting her husband in
his busy medical practice, helping scores of people
in her own right, playing hostess to countless guests
in her beautiful home and speaking at a variety of
meetings and church gatherings.

When I heard that she was to speak at the coffee
morning, I seized the opportunity to continue to
learn from her.

As usual, her face shone as she spoke about God.
I remember her face and demeanour more than her
words – except that she sowed that seed-thought
in my mind: that it is possible to encounter God
anywhere and everywhere. Coming from her, I knew
that these were not words borrowed from a text book
but rather a reality. So I sat up and took notice when

she recommended a little book which had helped to shape her prayer-life and I resolved to search for a copy of *The Practice of the Presence of God* by Brother Lawrence. Maybe I, too, would learn how to enjoy round-the-clock oneness with the Lord.

The Practice of the Presence of God

I found the book without difficulty, but reading it was far from easy. Perhaps this is not surprising since it was first published in 1693 in French and the copy I acquired was a reprint of the 1824 English edition. Even now, as I read the Preface, the stilted, antiquated language causes me to cringe:

> These letters are so edifying, so rich in unction, and have been found so full of delight by those who have had the joy of reading them, that the first readers have desired not to be alone in profiting by them. It is at their wish that the letters have been printed, for they judge that these writings will prove very useful to souls who are pressing forward to perfection by the practice of the presence of God.[1]

I tried hard to understand why my friend had recommended this book so highly. It was, after all, simply a two-part pocket-book. Part One consisted of a series of conversations which an impoverished, seventeenth-century monk had had over a period of some fifteen months with a certain Abbot: Joseph de Beaufort. This prominent church leader, having heard about Brother Lawrence's ability to find God everywhere, begged to be allowed to sit at his feet to discover his secret. Immediately after his sessions with Brother Lawrence, he recorded the monk's words in note form.

Part Two consists of sixteen of Brother Lawrence's letters. Six were written just two years before his death, four in the last four months of his life and two in the last month. All of them seem to have been addressed to people who had written to ask how they, too, could learn to enjoy God's presence in the stream of life.

Brother Lawrence seems to have been a reluctant correspondent. To one person he wrote:

> I cannot hide from you that it is with the utmost reluctance that I allow myself to yield to your importunities, and further [I only write] on this condition – that you show my letter to no one. If I knew that you felt obliged to show it, all the desire I have for your perfection would not induce me [to write].[2]

Despite this expressed embargo, the 'Reverend Mother' to whom he wrote evidently showed her letters to the Abbot who published them shortly after the monk's death. Unethical though this was, countless Christians down the centuries have been grateful for the Abbot's foresight.

I felt sure that the little book, coming from such a background, must contain hidden treasures, but they were so well concealed that I failed to see them. Since my children were young at the time, life afforded little opportunity to read and no time to dive deep enough into a book of this kind in the hope of dredging up even the richest of spiritual treasures.

Over the years, I would occasionally take the tiny,

yellow pocket-book from my shelves, dip into it and wonder why my friend loved it so much but still my unpractised eye failed to discern the spiritual pearls that lay buried in its sea-bed.

An invitation

Some thirty years later, my telephone rang and a familiar voice was asking me whether I would be prepared to speak on a certain date to the Women's Fellowship of the church which I then attended. Looking in my diary and noticing that the date was free, I agreed but my heart sank as I listened to the answer to my question: 'What would you like me to speak about?' 'Well, Joyce,' the caller was saying, 'we would really like you to talk about practising the presence of God. We thought you would have a lot to say on that subject.'

For some reason, I accepted the challenge. So the little yellow book saw the light of day once more, but this time, in order to interpret its contents for this group of women, I not only read it, I studied it. As I did so, the riches revealed themselves and I saw why my friend had recommended the little treatise all those years ago.

I wished that I had given myself more time to prepare this particular talk because I was learning so much from my research. I resolved to continue it beyond the meeting.

I did. It was then that I discovered another little gem written by Brother Lawrence: *The Spiritual Maxims*. Unlike the personal letters which were not intended for publication, it seems probable that these 'maxims' were intended for wide circulation –

even in book form. They seem to give a condensed, precise answer to the question the Abbot, the Reverend Mother and so many others were asking: How can *we* practice the presence of God? Here I found distilled wisdom and much food for meditation.

I also discovered an invaluable document written by the Abbot, shortly after the death of the monk: *The Character of Brother Lawrence.* This paints a fascinating pen portrait of the monk himself. For the purposes of this book, I have drawn on all four documents: the letters and conversations, the character and, in particular, the maxims. My aim has been four-fold: to present for my readers the kernel of Brother Lawrence's teaching, to attempt to interpret it so that today's busy Christians may discover for themselves where it impinges on their life-style, to show how Brother Lawrence's principles are firmly rooted in Scripture and to enthuse those who, like 'my' Women's Fellowship, yearn to discover for themselves the secret of finding God in life's fast lane. In addition to the reprint of the 1824 edition of *The Practice of the Presence of God* I have mentioned, and a copy of *The Spiritual Maxims*, published by Allenson, I have dipped, with appreciation and delight, into two new translations of the book: one by E.M. Blaiklock[3], the other by Louis Parkhurst.[4] I have also benefited enormously from the insights Robert Llewellyn shares in his introduction to *An Oratory of the Heart: Daily Readings with Brother Lawrence*[5], and I would recommend that readers who want to refer to the text might like to use these refreshing versions alongside the older translations.

In order to write this book with integrity, I felt that I should attempt to put into practice the practical suggestions Brother Lawrence gave to those who sought his help and guidance. At first I encountered difficulties which left me feeling frustrated and defeated. My love of silence is so great that finding God in the fast lane did not come naturally. But after applying myself to the practice of the presence of God for a period of some three years, I found that my perception of prayer and my experience of God was gradually being changed. More importantly, I was being changed by the prayer I was practising.

It was in New Zealand that I realised how much I had been changed. This book was finished, I had handed over the manuscript and I had only to read the proofs before publication. But just before I left Auckland after a hectic three and a half month tour, I visited a certain artist: Gael O'Leary. In her prayer-saturated studio hung a huge acrylic painting which seemed to sum up my prayer life powerfully and graphically.

The picture (illustrated on pages 16 and 17) was inviting me to celebrate the many facets of my life; to recognise that though, at times, they have me running round in circles, they also energise and shape me. The colours celebrate who I am, my vitality and life orchestrated by my Creator. As Gael explained:

"green celebrates the gift of life,
yellow and orange, hope and energy,
red, the driving power of love,
purples and mauves, suffering,
blue, the yearning for stillness, peace and God.

The off-centre blue square is a gentle reminder that we need 'time out' from our Martha-type existence to nourish the Mary within. Time to be still, to experience God in a different way. Time to listen; time to be loved; time to be re-energised with a strength beyond ourselves."

When we carve out times of stillness, we do not cease being creative, fulfilled and gifted, but we bring our concerns, loves, challenges, worries and questions into God's presence. These are represented by the swirling patterns in the blue square.

'Why a square?' someone asked when I showed them the prints of Gael's picture. Before I could respond, my questioner discovered her own answer. 'I suppose the straight lines surrounding all those swirls symbolise the need for discipline.' I liked that observation. Without discipline, we shall never reach the stage of pulling off the fast lane and into life's lay-bys.

My questioner reminded me of the retreatants who have heard me make mention of Brother Lawrence's insights on retreats and Quiet Days. Whenever I speak about finding God in the fast lane, the reaction always seems to be the same. Busy people prick up their ears and say with their eyes: 'Tell me more. Tell me how I can encounter God in the middle of the maelstrom.' The book starts with them, has been written for them and is in itself a prayer that they may learn to celebrate both stillness and busyness, recognise that God is to be found in both and dare to believe that, just as loving parents delight in the chaos which is introduced into their home with the arrival of children, so God, in a curious way, finds joy in us in the middle of our chaos and even uses it to transform us into his likeness.[7]

Joyce Huggett

CHAPTER 1

PRAYER 'ON THE HOOF'

'What mental picture does the phrase, "the fast lane" conjure up for you?' I once put that question to a group of women who had converged on Paris for a Quiet Day my husband and I were leading. 'For me, the key word is *rush*,' confessed one young mum. 'In Paris, the traffic rushes round me relentlessly. I rush to drop my children off at school before rushing on to work and this morning I rushed to catch the metro to come here.' As she spoke, several heads nodded. Clearly others identified with her interpretation of the phrase.

One woman after another then described the pictures the phrase conjured up for them before I confessed that, whenever I hear the words 'the fast lane', I see in my mind's eye, a young, ambitious, go-getting executive driving a powerful car along a motorway: head-lights on, foot hard on the accelerator, hand ready to grab the car phone, eyes ensuring no police car monitors his speed, mind racing, adrenalin flowing. Or I think of brief-case-clutching commuters being disgorged from over-crowded trains to race out of the station into the frantic world of finances and faxes, computers and constant phone-calls.

Some people I have spoken to think of hectic hospitals, broadcasters trying to beat the clock and journalists pushing themselves to meet impossible deadlines. Yet others sum up the situation with words rather than mental images: tension, stress, pressure, exhaustion, noise, deadlines are some of the words which spring to mind.

God and the fast lane

'Is it possible to find *God* in the fast lane?' That is a question a businessman who travelled daily to London once asked me: 'Can't you write a book which would help commuters to find God?' he challenged. A social worker threw down a similar gauntlet by placing the following question into the Question Box at a Social Workers' Retreat I was leading:

How is it possible to maintain inner stillness
when, in the office workplace -
phone ringing endlessly
interruptions
pressure
deadlines
crises
overwork
office politics
paper avalanche
cramped conditions
poor lighting
smoky atmosphere
work through lunch hour etc.
I know it is possible to get away e.g. lunch-
time. But is it possible to be still while IN the
maelstrom?

And a mother of three young off-spring who also acted as a foster mum for deprived or neglected children, when she attended a week of guided prayer[1] my husband and I were leading, begged to be shown how to experience God's presence in the middle of domestic chaos. I understood why when she showed me the diary she kept during a fairly typical week after accepting a social worker's invitation to foster two needy children under seven:

Monday
Sue refused to get dressed this morning. She screamed and threw a tantrum until it was time to go to school . . . When I looked at Jill I realised her blouse was inside out, her buttons fastened higgeldy piggeldy and that she was wearing odd socks . . .

Tuesday
Simon helpfully brought the milk in and dropped a pint which shattered all over the carpet. In the mayhem Phil forgot his swimming kit and lunch. Another extra trip before noon! Then Ann phoned. She had a class detention. Could I collect her at 4.00pm? . . .

The ironing pile is now totally out of control and erupting into the living room . . .

Just got home before Ken tonight to discover the cat or Mister Nobody had knocked one of the houseplants over spilling soil everywhere. Then, bang on tea time, a phone call from the social worker. 40 minutes later we sat down to eat.

Began to get the little ones ready for bed when Jill said: "Mummy Pat, my head is itchy." My heart sank. A frantic conveyor belt of heads bent over the bath was put in motion. Hair drenched in nit lotion then rinsed and towelled dry. Ken let the babysitter in and continued to spread and fill the sandwiches for the next day . . .

I think, too, of the doctors and nurses who attended a retreat my husband and I were leading. Was it possible, they queried, to be as conscious of the love of God in the cramped hospital quarters where they lived as they had been on retreat? Or would the sense of his presence evaporate when they returned overseas to the under-staffed, ill-equipped hospital where they worked?

The good news is that God *can* be found in the fast lane. His presence and his love are as available to us when we are besieged by busyness as they are when we pull into a quiet lay-by to contemplate him. To discover how to find him in the fast lane we turn in a seemingly unlikely direction – to the teaching and example of a seventeenth-century cook for whom Jesus' haunting promise: 'I am with you always' (Matt 28:20) became a minute-by-minute reality.

Brother Lawrence

The name of the cook was Nicholas Herman, better known as Brother Lawrence, inspirer of a little book entitled: *The Practice of the Presence of God.*

History records very little about this monk except that he was born of humble parents in Lorraine, in eastern France, around 1611.

Life in Lorraine at that time was particularly

precarious because France was at war with Germany. Civilian homes were constantly pillaged and destroyed and fear of homelessness was rife. It was an unsettling time for a youth to grow up.

The Thirty Years War continued into his teens, when he joined the army. Here, doubtless, his eyes were opened to further obscenities and degradation. Yet it was while he was still in his teens that he experienced an unforgettable, life-changing, encounter with God. His Damascus-road-type conversion took place as he stood and gazed at a fruit tree which 'spoke' to him more eloquently than any sermon. The tree was naked – stripped of all its leaves. Yet, he reflected, when winter gave way to spring, virgin green leaves would unfold. Later, flowers and then fruit would adorn the now-bare branches.

Just as the Psalmist once wrote, 'The heavens are proclaiming the glory of God' (Psalm 19:1), so Brother Lawrence used to delight to recall how this annual miracle of nature persuaded him that God is good and majestic, powerful and all-loving. The all-consuming, reciprocal love with which he was filled while he gazed at this tree changed the direction of his life. From that day on he discovered his life's goal – to live for God: 'I want only him and to be all his.'[2]

Throughout the rest of his life, like Jesus, he allowed the ordinary things around him to remind him of the God who cannot be seen but who can be known and loved; the God who always enfolds us in love.

After eighteen years in the army, he sustained a severe leg wound when Swedish soldiers raided his native village of Rambervilliers. Defying death and the threat of blood-poisoning and gangrene, he recovered. But, owing to a permanent limp, he was invalided out of the army. After a period of convalescence with his parents, he became footman to a William de Fuibert, treasurer of the Exchequer – a disastrous appointment for a self-confessed 'great awkward fellow who broke everything'.[3]

This clumsiness, which doubtless resulted in best china being broken and precious glassware being smashed, drove him to seek admission to the Carmelite Monastery in Paris. There he trusted that God would punish him and make him smart for his awkwardness and other faults. Instead, from the moment of entry, he testifies that, in the monastery, he found 'nothing but contentment'[4] even though he was given the exacting and responsible task of working in the monastery kitchen – the equivalent of one of the monastery's fast lanes.

Many people would not put the words fast lane and monastery or convent together. They seem incompatible. The antithesis of each other. But the rhythm of the monastic day stretches many monks and nuns – especially in the early days. As one monk explains:

Our day is a full one. It starts at 2.15am. We go to the church for night-office or vigils, as we call it; this means twenty to forty-five minutes given to psalm recitation or singing interspersed with readings . . . The chief ingredients of our life are prayer and reading, study and work.[5]

This monk goes on to explain that the early morning service of vigils is followed by the Eucharist. When this service is over, the monks linger in the chapel for a period of silent reflection and thanksgiving before taking their first meal of the day: breakfast.

Between breakfast and the next service (5.30am), the monks are free to wash, shave, study and enjoy some 'spiritual reading'. At 6.00am, as soon as the 5.30am service is over, manual work begins. Some will milk the cows, others will look after the sheep, yet others will deal with the laundry, work in the kitchen or elsewhere in the monastery, its gardens or its farm.

This manual work continues until 11.00am. Another short service punctuates the busyness of the morning and lunch. Everyone helps to wash up and clean the kitchen before taking a siesta or enjoying a brief spell of free time: reading, writing or praying.

The next service takes place at 1.30 and, as soon as it is over, the manual work begins again. It continues until the late afternoon service of Vespers. Supper follows Vespers and community discussions and relaxation fill the period between supper and the last service of the day: Compline. At 7.30pm, as soon as the psalms of Compline have been sung and the blessing pronounced, the monks may retire to their room. As this monk wryly reflects: 'It may seem a ridiculously early hour to go to bed but you soon find that rising at 2.15am leaves you quite unattracted to staying up late'[6].

If the day feels full for all the monks, it must feel extra full for the monastery cook who is responsible for ensuring that the first meal of the day is ready immediately after the Eucharist.

Breakfast, like all meals, coming so close to the end of a service, will only be ready on time if careful forethought and punctilious preparation result in split-second timing when the meal is being served. This task is made doubly difficult because visitors may arrive unannounced and be invited to eat with the monks so the cook never knows precisely how many people he is feeding at any given time.

I think of an occasion when I was staying in a convent where the nuns' daily time-table resembled the time-table I have just described. As usual, after the midday service, the nuns, the retreatants and an unexpected guest made their way from the chapel to the refectory. There we stood observing the obligatory silence and waiting for the Mother Superior to say grace. Grace was never said until the food appeared. No food came. So we waited and waited and waited – still standing. No words passed our lips but as eyebrows were raised and watches examined, the level of embarrassment rose with every tick of the refectory clock. Eventually, a flustered nun rushed through the swing doors clutching two vegetable dishes. Her undignified entry, flushed face and despairing eyes expressed shame and profuse apologies. Grace was duly said, lunch began and I realised that the kitchen is, indeed, one of the convent's fast lanes.

Brother Lawrence's description of the monastery kitchen often reminds me of that day at the convent. He uses words like rush, bustle and clatter and implies that it would be normal for several people at once to clamour for his attention while he was in the middle of his own work. His lameness, his aversion to cooking and the constant pressure could have caused him to lose the serenity for which he became well-known and envied. Instead he could claim that he had learned to 'pray on the hoof':

> The time of busyness does not differ with me from the time of prayer: and in the noise and clatter of my kitchen, while several persons are

at the same time calling for different things, I possess God in as great tranquillity as if I were on my knees.[7]

Equally, he claimed that he encountered God while cobbling the monks' shoes and while on business trips. One of his responsibilities was to buy the monastery's supply of wine which involved travelling by boat from Paris to Burgundy and Auvergne and bringing back with him barrels of wine. He disliked these trips partly because of his lack of business acumen and partly because his lameness restricted his mobility – he could move about the boat only by rolling himself over the wine casks. Even so we find him rejoicing in God's intervention in these potentially irksome transactions. He simply asked God to partner him, trusted that he would do so and watched to see how all the details would be woven into a beautiful pattern.

Like Paul he seemed to be able to say with integrity: 'I am ready for anything anywhere . . . There is nothing I cannot master with the One who gives me strength.'[8]

Let ordinary things point you to God

The question for the businessman and the social worker, the foster mum and the missionary medics I mentioned at the beginning of this chapter is: How did he do it? It is the question which has inspired this book. For it is a question which many people put to Brother Lawrence during his life-time. His serenity and sense of wellbeing in the middle of chaos did not pass unnoticed. It shone through him so effectively that Parisians from all sections of society flocked to him to learn his secret. Those who observed him claimed that:

> his very countenance was edifying . . . in the greatest hurry of business in the kitchen he still preserved his recollection and heavenly-mindedness. He was never hasty nor loitering, but did each thing in its season with an even, uninterrupted composure and tranquillity of spirit.[9]

His reputation and example were so powerful that his biographer claimed of him:

> Though it was in a very lowly corner that Brother Lawrence lived his days, yet there is no person, of whatsoever station or condition he be, who may not draw great profit from his life. Those who are filled with the cares of this world he will teach to draw near to God, to ask from Him the grace to do their duty faithfully, never forgetting that they can approach God, when they are most busied, in the market and where men do congregate or in the hour of leisure.[10]

In other words the secret of his serenity was simple. It sprang from recognising that we may encounter God everywhere. 'God is everywhere, in all places and there is no spot where we cannot draw near to Him, and hear Him speaking in our heart: with a little *love*, just a very little, we shall not find it hard.'[11]

For today's over-stretched, over-stimulated, pressurised people, this news sounds almost too good to

be true. We are tempted to ask whether the monk is exaggerating when he claims that 'Whoever practices God's presence will soon become spiritual.'[12]
Yet he insists:

Were I a preacher, I should above all other things preach the practice of the presence of God. And were I a Spiritual Director, I would advise all the world to it – so necessary do I think it to be and so easy too ... I cannot imagine how religious persons can live satisfied without the practice of the presence of God.[13]

And, of course, he is not alone in claiming that we can encounter God anywhere and everywhere. Christians down the centuries have reiterated this claim. As David Adam has shown in his series of books on prayer, this philosophy lay at the heart of the spirituality of Celtic Christians.

There was from them a Divine Immanence that helped them to transcend much that was dull routine and hard labour. They talked naturally to God as a man or woman talks to a friend. They rejoiced in a closeness and were sure of His help. Through Him, a glory was theirs, a glory that made the world quite a different place, for they were never alone. Whether they needed guidance, a helping hand or a companion, they could turn to the Friend and say, "God".[14]

Draw on God's grace

In addition to encouraging would-be disciples to recognise that ordinary, mundane things can remind us of God, the monk reminds us that we cannot practice the presence of God in our own strength. Such prayer is a gift. A gift of grace. All that is required of us is that we should receive from God this free, undeserved love-gift. 'We should in all confidence ask for his grace . . . relying only on the infinite merits of our Lord. God never fails to offer his grace at every juncture.'[15]

Those who most readily ask are those who are grafted into God and who acknowledge their dependence on him for everything. 'How can we be with Him, unless our thoughts are ever of Him? How can He be in our thoughts, unless we form a holy habit of abiding in His Presence, there asking for the grace we need each moment of our life?'[16]

Here, as throughout his teaching, Brother Lawrence reflects many of the memorable, pithy sayings of Jesus: 'Ask and it will be given to you . . .' (Matt 7:7) and 'If you remain in me and my words remain in you, ask whatever you wish, and it will be given you.' (John 15:7)

His teaching on grace is shot through with sentiments dear to the apostles. Luke, for example, underlines that we believe by grace (Acts 18:27), while Paul stresses that we are saved by grace (Eph 2:8), we minister by grace (Eph 3:8) and we are what we are by the grace which is poured on us in great abundance. (1 Cor 15:10 and 1 Tim 1:14)

The importance of this word 'grace' was underlined for me while I was writing this book. Faced with a choice of continuing to live and work in England or offering to work for the church overseas,

I went on retreat in an attempt to discover God's hopes and expectations for my future. As I prayed and reflected, the call to live and work overseas crystalised. I could not ignore it, neither did I want to. I longed to be able to say a glad and ready yes. Yet, to my dismay, I found that, in my own strength, I was quite incapable of making such a costly, calculated choice. Eventually the proverbial penny dropped and I realised that, of myself, I do not possess the resources to make such a sacrifice even for God. 'I need your grace to help me to say "yes"' was the prayer I whispered one night as I was falling asleep. In the middle of that night, during a wakeful but peaceful hour, I found welling up inside me the resounding yes I had been struggling to squeeze out for several weeks. It was a humbling but joyful moment in which a profound truth was embedded in my heart: *everything* is grace. Pure gift.

I suspect that John Ford, a life member of the Bible Reading Fellowship, was gripped by a similar realisation while he was meditating on *The Practice of the Presence of God*; that this realisation prompted this prayer:

Dearest Father in heaven,
because of your grace,
the infection of Jesus
and the power of the Holy spirit,
a very ordinary domestic servant
became extraordinarily aware of your presence.
Grant me the grace
to experience the joys of true awareness
of your presence
that I may go about my daily tasks
in joyful harmony with you.[17]

For personal reflection

1. If you feel you can, echo that prayer.

2. Or write your own prayer asking God for the grace to encounter him 'on the hoof'.

3. Brother Lawrence's life-goal clarified in his late teens. It was to live for God. Ask yourself: What is the goal of my life? What am I doing to guarantee that I reach this goal? Does my life-style help or hinder my journey?

4. Ask yourself two more penetrating questions: When am I most conscious of the ever-enfolding love of God?
   When am I least conscious of God's presence and love?

5. Do *you* approach God at the peak of your busyness or only when you have time to stop and 'just be'? If so, why?

6. Close your eyes, look back over the past twenty-four hours and watch an action replay of the events of the past day and night. As the memories surface, home in only on the good things that have happened to you. Relive them in your imagination. Relish them. Enjoy them. Recognise them for what they are: signs of God's encompassing, attentive love and give him thanks.

CHAPTER 2

SETTING LONG-TERM GOALS

Two things are necessary for those who determine to find God in the fast lane as well as in the lay-by. The first is the recognition that they cannot do it in their own strength and they therefore stretch out empty hands to receive the free gift of God's grace. The second is that they set themselves the task of praying on the hoof by practising the presence of God.

'But what does practising the presence of God mean?' a harrassed retreatant once asked me when she noticed that I planned to speak on the subject during the course of her retreat.

Drawing on his own experience and that of a fellow monk, Brother Lawrence gave several succinct definitions of the phrase. It means, amongst other things:

'a directing of our spirit to God,'[1]
'a remembrance of God which can come about either through the imagination or the mind',[2]
'an alertness towards God
a wordless conversation with him,
confidence in him.'[3]
It also involves:
paying God 'simple attention',[4]
recognising that we have a prayer place in our heart[5],

acknowledging that God is nearer to us than we can ever imagine,[6]
Thinking of him perpetually.[7]

In other words, practising the presence of God simply means to be attentive, however momentarily, of the truth of Acts 17:27–28 that God is never far from any of us. In him we live and move and have our being. It is an awareness of and an in-tuneness with his loving presence.

I sometimes think of it in this way. Now that I am living overseas, I seem to have a deep need to keep in touch with England so I am grateful that the World Service of the BBC transmits regular programmes throughout the day and night. All I have to do is to tune my radio and I am connected to the homeland.

God similarly transmits messages at all times – messages of unending love. To connect ourselves to this love, we need only fine-tune our hearts and minds to be aware of it. Then, no matter what we are doing, we can be drawn into deep mysteries: that God exists, that love is what he is, that he cares about us, that he is always working on our behalf, that he stooped to enter our world – stooped to enter our lives: that he indwells us. As David Adam puts it, 'we may vibrate to' his Presence.[8]

Living concurrently

The Quaker Thomas Kelly calls this equal alertness to the sacred and the secular 'living concurrently'.

He claims that we can train ourselves to be equally aware of the world in which we live and of God's presence. Likening us to the tortoise, he throws out this challenge: 'The tortoise swims about in the waters of the lake, but her mind is fixed to where her eggs are laid on the bank. So, do all the work of the world, but keep your mind in God.'9

This concept inspired me when I was attending a Communion Service on one occasion. The service had scarcely begun when a little friend of mine aged nearly three decided that she would prefer my company to her mother's. So I spent the entire service living concurrently. On one level I was paying careful attention to Miriam's quiet (and not so quiet) chatter, drawing pictures for her, reading to her. On another level, my attention remained fully on the liturgy. The two experiences did not vie with each other. They dovetailed and even fed each other.

A few days later, another incident reminded me that many of us spend most of our time living concurrently. I was exploring another author's experience of the practice of the presence of God when the telephone rang. I listened to the caller, made my response, then returned to the research I had been engaged in. Some ten minutes later I realised that I was doing two things at once: assimilating the content of the book I was reading and turning over and over in my mind a few phrases from the telephone conversation.

In a similar vein, most of us spend much of our time thinking, even talking to ourselves – as we walk, as we work, as we fall asleep, as we wake – particularly when we are angry or anxious. Since this is so, tuning in to the ever-present love of God demands little more than a re-channelling of this ceaseless chatter so that we talk to the indwelling God as well as to ourselves.

Finding God everywhere

In *Dialogue With God*, Mark Virkler describes how he has worked at this life-changing discipline so that now, as he drives, he worships: 'I share love with Jesus, I sing Him a love song and allow Him to speak back to me in spontaneous thoughts.'[10]

It took a personal crisis to convince the contemporary writer, Sue Monk Kidd that God comes to us in the ordinary things of life. In *God's Joyful Surprise* she allows us to peep through the window of her own life:

Every day the nearness of God collected in me like rain water. I sensed Him coming and coming and coming . . . in a sound, a smell, a touch, a movement, in common things that shaped my day . . . I would stare at the most mundane things and be aware of His love. A pitcher of milk in the refrigerator, an old sweater, the steam rising off my soup, a quiet sky, an uprooted tree . . . all were gifts of love.

"Enjoy. Drink Me in," [God] seemed to say. "Find My love everywhere!" . . .

She describes how, one day, she stood mesmerized by 'the silent floating beauty' of a hot air balloon sailing over her home – by the fullness that held it aloft . . .

I was deeply touched by the presence of God and His love in that moment . . . I came inside and scrawled in my journal, "God, if I could only wake up and pay attention to things as they really are, I would see that Your presence fills this world like a hot air balloon."[11]

These authors have not suddenly stumbled on a new dimension of spirituality. They have simply woken up to the fact that when Jesus said, 'I will never leave you', he meant it. Christians down the ages have similarly become acutely conscious of his all-encompassing, ever-embracing, never-failing love. Take the Celtic Christians for example. They perceived God as the One who pervaded everything so they expected to encounter him in their workplace and on their travels. Their prayers reveal that their senses were like antennae – ever alert and ready to detect the presence of the All-powerful, Invisible One whom they expected to meet when fishing or farming, dressing or eating, waking or falling asleep. They assumed and gave thanks for his presence at the birth of their babies and rested in the confidence that he would still be with them in the moment of death. He was real.[12] That is why they could produce delightful prayers for every imaginable occasion. Like this comprehensive one:

God In All

In your walking – God
In your talking – God
In your life – God
In your strife – God
In your seeing – God

In your being   – God
In your days   – God
In your ways   – God
In your night   – God
In your plight – God
In your reason – God
In every season – God

With God I'm bound
All around.[13]

Since Christians down the ages seem to have established the fact that practising the presence of God is not a pipedream but the norm, we need to address ourselves to a key question: How can over-stretched, over-stimulated, stressed twentieth-century Christians enjoy the constant kind of communion with God summed up by Brother Ramon and David Adams:

In You, my Lord, I live
                and move
                and have my being.

In me, my Lord, You live
                and move
                and have Your being.[14]

God is in all the world and waits to be discovered there – or, to be more exact, the world is in Him, all is in the heart of God. Our work, our travels, our joys and sorrows are enfolded in His loving care. We cannot for a moment fall out of the hands of God. Typing pool and workshop, office and factory are all as sacred as the church. The Presence of God pervades the work place as much as He does a church sanctuary.[15]

An accurate image of God

For guidance we turn back to Brother Lawrence. When we do so, we notice how vital it is to set ourselves long-term goals, the first of which must be to establish within our hearts an accurate image of God.

For this reason, at the beginning of a retreat, I often invite retreatants to draw a picture or diagram which sums up for them the way they perceive God. Brother Lawrence might have drawn a man wearing a crown because he describes God as a King who is full of mercy and goodness. This King,

> embraces me with love, makes me eat at His table, serves me with His own hands, gives me the key of His treasures; He converses and delights Himself with me incessantly, in a thousand and a thousand ways, and treats me in all respects as His favourite.[16]

Life, for Brother Lawrence, was unwrapping the King's gifts, relishing his love, abandoning himself to that love as a surfer abandons himself to the surge of the sea. Life also involved responding to the divine lavishness, abundance and extravagance by humble, hidden service and deep-down confidence. As his biographer expressed it:

> The high notion which he had of God revealed in his heart a perfect picture of his Creator in all His Sovereign Justice and Infinite Mercy. Resting on this he was assured that God would never deceive him and would send such things only as were good for him.[17]

A responsive love

Such confidence and awareness of God's love draws from the believer a reciprocal love. Since this, in turn, gives birth to a desire to bring joy to the Beloved by serving him, we need to see it as another of our long-term goals.

This was underlined for me by a friend of mine whose love for God had grown cold until she went on a retreat. There, while meditating on the story of the lost sheep, her love was rekindled as she found herself being lifted, in her imagination, on the shoulders of the Good Shepherd who seemed to delight to hold her close to his cheek. 'All day, it's as though his love has been wrapped round me like a cloak,' she told me. And now I really want to serve him.

She *was* serving him, albeit by performing menial, uncongenial tasks in the hiddenness of a Christian community. But whereas before the retreat she had performed these tasks dutifully because they needed to be done, now she tackled them joyfully and purposefully, as though she were doing them for God himself. It was as though the orientation of her life had changed. She was no longer concerned about herself. Jesus' motto became hers also: 'I have come to do your will, O God.' (Heb 10:7) As I watched her at work, I saw her take on something of the stunning beauty and majesty of a ship sailing straight for the harbour and I knew that her harbour was God.

Brother Lawrence would have been thrilled by the change in her because, in one of his conversations with one of his disciples, he made this observation: 'We must not grow weary in doing little things for the love of God, who looks not to the greatness of the deed, but to the love.'[18]

On another occasion, he admitted to the same person: 'I took on a monk's life only for the love of God. I have sought only to live for him . . . It is my desire to go on living purely for the love of God.'[19]

Make sure your life revolves around God

He also gave this gentle challenge: 'Consider God as the goal of all your thoughts and desires.'[20]

Indeed, he starts his little treatise *The Spiritual Maxims* with this extravagant claim: Believers who 'look always to God and his glory in all that we do, say and undertake' are on the path to perfection.[21]

I was thinking about this aspect of his teaching

one day as I travelled by train from Tel Aviv to Jerusalem. My husband was travelling with his back to the engine and recalling nostagically the people we had met and the fellowship we had enjoyed in Tel Aviv. I, on the other hand, faced the way we were going: to Jerusalem. A thrill ran through me as the hills surrounding the city came in sight. I imagined the pilgrims of old approaching 'the Holy City' praising God by chanting celebratory psalms. And I thought of Jesus who 'set his face like a flint' towards this city even though he knew that this was the place where he would be mugged and murdered by those he had come to save. And I realised that it is possible to be travelling towards God in one of two ways: facing the way we are travelling, full of joy, anticipation and commitment, or reluctantly, even begrudgingly – with our back to the engine, as it were, and our hearts and affections centred on people, places and primarily on ourselves.

Brother Lawrence stressed that, if we want to practice the presence of God, like Jesus, we must face the way we are travelling: 'Your only business in this life is to please God . . . Employ your life in loving and serving God, who by His mercy has called you for that very purpose.'[22]

He himself, from the day he felt overwhelmed by the divine love while gazing at the bare branches of a fruit tree in winter, 'fixed his gaze on God alone, the Goal of his race, and *sped* along towards Him by daily acts . . . of love.'[23]

He could claim: 'I have looked on God as the *Goal* and *End* of all the thoughts and affections of the soul.'[24]

His biographer, the Abbot from Beaufort, records that towards the end of his first session with him, the monk underlined that if he could promise this wholehearted, love-inspired commitment, he would continue to teach him how to practice the presence of God. If, however, he was not prepared to pay the price, he should not return to the monastery.

The Abbot did return and continued to beg the saintly monk to reveal his secret. How had he learned to practice the presence of God? How could the Abbot enjoy a similar relationship? In response, over and over again, he received a variation on this theme of commitment. By way of explanation Brother Lawrence simply said: 'I have come to see that my only business is to live as though there were none but He and I in the world,'[25] and 'I have sought only to live for him.'[26]

Living for his King had affected Brother Lawrence's entire life so that he had learned to do even the most mundane task for God – like taking up 'a straw from the ground . . . seeking Him only and nothing else, not even His gifts'.[27]

And even though he had a great aversion to the work he had been assigned in the monastery kitchen, he had learned 'to do everything there for the love of God'.[28] He lived in constant 'readiness to lay down his life for the love of God'.[29]

The letters he wrote to another enquirer, 'the Reverend Mother', reiterate this foundational principle. In his very first letter to her he expresses his frustration with the books on prayer he had read which offered him a whole variety of methods of approaching God but failed to teach him the lesson he most wanted to learn: 'how to become wholly God's'.[30] Eventually he had unearthed the secret: 'to give the all for the all'.[31]

Hundreds of years later, Joy Davidman, wife of

C.S.Lewis, put it this way: 'to want God so much that everything else becomes irrelevant'.[32]

The fifth-century Isaac of Stella expressed the same goal poetically and beautifully:

> He himself is my contemplation;
> He is my delight.
> Him for his own sake
> I seek above me.
> From him himself
> I feed within me.
> He is the field
> In which I labour.
> He is the food
> For which I labour.
> He is my cause
> He is my effect
> He is my beginning
> He is my end, without end.
> He is for me
> Eternity.[33]

I was attempting to make my own response to this high calling one morning while my husband and I were driving to the beach. The car rounded a bend when we discovered that the vehicle in front of us had stopped abruptly. We soon saw the reason. A herd of goats was crossing the road, their sleek bodies gleaming in the sun. They were followed by the goat-herd. As we watched and waited, I saw that, while most of the goats had reached their destination: a plateau with a few welcome strands of greenery still growing, some stragglers still remained in the road while others stubbornly strayed on the other side. These were being rounded-up by an Alsatian.

The scene helped me to understand why one part
of me seems prepared to pay the high price of discipleship we have been considering while another
part of me hesitates. We are complex beings. We
make a commitment to Christ which matches the
life-changing U-turn made by Brother Lawrence
when he gave his life to God. For a while we feel
full of enthusiasm. Nothing and no-one can dissuade
us from sacrificing self for the sake of the Kingdom.
Then we cringe at the cost and wonder why. The reason is that, like the sensible goats who went straight
to the green pastures, certain parts of our personality concur wholeheartedly with the commitment we
have made. That part of us had been captivated by
Christ so that even though serving him takes us
through a personal Gethsemane and a living death,
we refuse to turn back. Other parts of our personality, however, are more like the stragglers. These
rebel or sluggish parts of ourselves need to be infused

by the Holy Spirit so that, infected by love, they also gradually turn away from self and towards Christ. Because the process is gradual and not immediate, we need to be as patient with ourselves as Jesus is. That is why I find a far-reaching prayer of St Ignatius of particular value and importance: 'Lord, turn my *whole being* to your praise and glory.'

Determine to persevere

When, eventually, all the goats were rounded up, we reached the beach. It was only 8.00am but a family had already settled in our favourite spot in the shade of the rocks. The father was teaching his daughter to swim. From the water, we watched him stand on the shore shouting instructions which the girl obeyed. After a while, there was nothing more for him to say. He had taught her all he could. Now it was up to her to practice.

She splashed around in the shallows while we swam but after an interval of some twenty-five minutes we heard the man calling us, begging us to watch his pupil. His ear-to-ear grin expressed his own pleasure at her progress and, with equal delight, we joined in his applause. Practice was improving her performance by the minute as she learned to abandon her body to the buoyant waters of the Mediterranean.

Practice is also the only thing that will perfect our ability to keep in touch with the ever-present, in-dwelling God. Brother Lawrence reminds us of this in *The Spiritual Maxims* where he urges us to display: 'a great faithfulness in the *practice* of this presence and in keeping the soul's gaze on God.'[34]

He underlined this, too, when he met with the Abbot for the first time. There is a great need for perseverance and 'fidelity in prayer even in those times of dryness or sluggishness or weariness by which God tries your love for him.'[35]

He repeated the sentiment during the Abbot's second visit: 'A little perseverance, he said, was needed at first to form the habit of conversing all the time with God and referring all actions to Him. However, after a little care one felt stirred by his love without any trouble.'[36]

Similarly, in response to a letter 'The Reverend Mother N' seems to have written asking how she might emulate the monk, he wrote:

I cannot understand how women in religious communities can live content without the practice of the presence of God. For my part I keep myself apart with him, at the depth and centre of my soul as much as I am able . . . You must buffet yourself. At the outset one often feels that it is a waste of time, but you must go on and determine to persevere therein to death in spite of all the difficulties.[37]

On another occasion he wrote encouragingly on the subject of wandering thoughts:

My . . . Most Honoured Mother,
You tell me nothing new. You are not the only one to be troubled by your thoughts. Our mind is always given to roving . . . I believe that the cure for this is to confess all our faults and to humble ourselves before God. I do not advise you to much talking at prayer, for much talking

is often an occasion for wandering. Hold yourself before God like a poor dumb person, or a paralytic at a rich man's gate. Give your attention to keeping your mind in the presence of the Lord. If it wanders and withdraws at times, do not be disturbed. To trouble the mind serves more often to distract than to recall it. The will must call it back quietly. If you persevere in this, God will have pity on you.[38]

That reassuring phrase: 'God will have pity on you' took on a new meaning for me while I was writing this chapter. It happened while I was listening to a lecture on how to learn a foreign language. The lecturer was an American who had set himself the task of mastering Arabic. As he shared with us a method which had helped him, I found myself fascinated by the reaction of an Arab who was sitting in on the lecture. From time to time, as the American tried to pronounce sounds which seem almost impossible to a Westerner's vocal chords, he would chuckle out loud. At the same time his face was alight with delight making it clear that by his laughter he was not criticising the strong, strident, American accent but rather he was attempting to express admiration and approval. He was cheering the budding linguist on, wanting him to master the impossible.

Brother Lawrence seems to encourage us to believe that God is like that – not so much troubled by our many mistakes as eager to applaud us every step of the way as we learn the difficult art of growing in our awareness that his love enfolds us every moment of every day and every night:

We must go on working, for in the life of the

spirit not to go on is to lose ground. Those who have the mind of the Holy Spirit, sail on, even when they are asleep. If the small ship of our soul is still beaten by the winds and the storm, let us awaken the Lord who sleeps in it, and he will soon calm the sea.[39]

If today's commuter and nurse, young mum, busy social worker and other pressurised Christians who want to learn the practice of the presence of God are to make progress in this kind of jubilant prayer, they must take note of the long-term goals mentioned in this chapter:

- ensure that their image of God is accurate in that it reflects the picture of God painted in the Bible.
- allow their hearts to be so warmed and touched by God's love that they find welling up inside of themselves a reciprocal love.
- ensure that their life is increasingly revolving around God and not around self, recognising that he is the reason for our existence. (As Paul puts it, we were chosen to be children of God: chosen to bring pleasure to him by being with him and chosen to bring glory to him in everything we do.)
- determine to persevere in the practice of the presence of God remembering that the grace of God is always freely available:

When [God] finds a soul imbued with living faith, into it he pours grace on grace, a flowing stream, as it were. . . .
We often check this torrent by the small

regard we have for it. Let us check it no more . . .
let us return into ourselves, break down this
dam, make open the way for grace, and make
up for lost time.[40]

For personal reflection:

1. Draw a picture or diagram which sums up
   your perception of God. Consider, among other
   things, that Jesus depicted God as a Good
   Shepherd searching for a lost sheep, a middle-
   eastern woman hunting for a lost coin and a
   compassionate father. (Luke 15)

2. Look back over your life and trace the way
   God's love has protected you from harm, given
   you joy and drawn you to himself.

3. Look back over your life and recall occasions
   when God was clearly the centre of your universe. Compare those times with the present
   and pray the prayer of St Ignatius:
   'Lord, turn my whole being to your praise
   and glory.'

4. Think of ways in which you 'live concurrently'. Let them inspire you to find God in
   the fast lane.

5. If someone asked you: 'What is your life's
   motto?' what would you say?

6. Think of your self travelling towards God in
   a train, as described in this chapter. Would

you say you are facing the engine or travelling with your back to it? Talk to God about this realisation.

7. Brother Lawrence claimed that he did everything for God. Think of the demands that claim your time day by day. How can you learn to do these for God?

8. Ask God for the grace to persevere in learning to fine-tune yourself to his presence – perhaps using this Celtic prayer:

>Awaken me, Lord
>To your light,
>Open my eyes
>To your presence.
>
>Awaken me, Lord
>To your love,
>Open my heart
>To your indwelling.
>
>Awaken me, Lord
>To your life,
>Open my mind
>To your abiding.
>
>Awaken me, Lord
>To your purpose,
>Open my will
>To your guiding.[41]

CHAPTER 3

SETTING SHORT-TERM GOALS

Brother Lawrence likens practising the presence of God to setting out on a journey. The adventure begins, as we saw in the last chapter, by setting long-term goals – that is, establishing our ultimate destination and planning the route to ensure that we will reach it eventually. When we do this, the path ahead becomes clear.

The Christian's destination is God. Travelling towards him may well be hard at times. We therefore need to persevere and to avail ourselves of the readily-available, minute-by-minute grace he always gives to those who trust him enough to stretch out empty hands to him. Brother Lawrence suggests that, in addition to setting ourselves long-term goals, there are other practical measures we can take to ensure that no matter what obstacles are placed in our way, we progress slowly but steadily in a God-ward direction.

I was rehearsing some of these one hot, summer's day while my husband and I were climbing in the Troodos mountains in Cyprus. The going was rough because the path was stony, and tough because the terrain was steep. 'Just like practising the presence of God', I thought. I was feeling frustrated that day because I was finding that, even though I was studying Brother Lawrence's philosophy, and attempting to put into practice the principles I was unearthing, whole days could flash by and at the end of them I would realise that I had forgotten to tune into the ever present love of God.

As I climbed, suddenly, to my great relief, I stumbled on some steps which someone had cut into the path and which made the climb not only possible but comparatively easy. Suddenly, I realised that these short-term goals could be like stepping-stones helping us to cross from the bank of our familiar ways of prayer to the unexplored territory on the other side of the stream.

Refuse to be discouraged

That day, I needed to remind myself of a vitally important prayer principle. Brother Lawrence spells it out in *The Spiritual Maxims*: 'Be not disheartened at your many falls; truly this habit can only be formed with difficulty.'[1]

This step was obviously cut out of the bitterness of personal experience, for, with disarming honesty, he confesses that for the first ten years of his apprenticeship in practising the presence of God, he experienced a series of disheartening set backs:

> During the first ten years I suffered much. The apprehension I had of not belonging to God as I should have wished, my past sins always present before my eyes, and the goodness of God to me, were the material and the source of my woes. During this time I often fell . . . It seemed to me that man, reason, and even God were against me, and that faith alone was for me.[2]

Yet he goes on to explain that when he fell or when he

recalled that he had been unmindful of the presence of God, he quickly picked himself up again and that, after years of frustration, he found that practising the presence of God became a habit which gave him much joy. He suggests to those of us whose desire to discover his secret is strong that we should do the same. And he offers a series of other practical suggestions.

Pray before attempting any task

The first is reminiscent of Paul's teaching: 'Pray all the time, asking for what you need.' (Eph 6:18) Brother Lawrence puts it this way: 'Talk to God about everything. Seek his help before attempting even the most mundane task.'[3]

When *he* was about to begin work, he would pray a simple, straightforward prayer like this one:

O my God, since Thou art with me, and I must now, in obedience to Thy commands, apply my mind to these outward things, I beseech Thee to grant me the grace to continue in Thy presence; and to this end do Thou prosper me with Thy assistance, receive all my works, and possess all my affections.[4]

Having prayed such a prayer, he opened himself to receive the strength he needed 'and more besides'.

This system worked so well that, with great confidence, he encouraged others to use it. But does it work for us today, in our busy, frenetic, materialistic society? I was still asking myself this question while my husband and I were leading a retreat overseas.

We would meet as a group each morning, discover together the riches of Bible meditation, then individually they would spend time pondering a scripture passage on their own. Later each individual would meet with David or myself and share with us the fruit of their prayer-time.

One of my retreatants had undertaken to cook lunch for all of us so I used to meet with her first. As soon as she left me, I knew that she would be busy working in the kitchen and so I felt anxious lest her busyness should spoil her stillness with God. With this in mind, I used to pray with her before she left me that, like Brother Lawrence, she would be as aware of the presence of God while cooking as she was when she was meditating in her own room.

One day, I asked her whether being the cook was interrupting her retreat. She looked surprised by my question and replied with a genuine: 'Oh no! While I'm preparing the lunch, I talk to the Lord and he carries on talking to me.'

Her bright smile and jubilant testimony prompted me to examine the reasons why many of us fail to experience a similar sense of God's presence in our place of work. One reason is that, when faced with an avalanche of paperwork or a pile of nappies, a deadline to meet or a telephone which rings incessantly, it is easy to forget that God even exists let alone remember to talk to him. As a Christian completing his period of military service once put it: 'My time in the army has been so pressurised that I feel as though I've been *enslaved* with time scarcely able to think about God let alone talk to him.' Or, as David Goodall, writing in *The Tablet* admits:

I know from experience that unless I can find

time to advert regularly, consciously and specifically to God's presence and seek some kind of dialogue with him, the whole supernatural dimension, the reality of the unseen life of the spirit, begins to fade ... This afternoon's meeting, the telegram of instructions that must be acted on, Parliamentary Questions that must be answered ... the pleasures and pressures of ordinary living ... take over.[5]

Another reason why some of us fail to tune in to God's ever-available love is that we are so accustomed to taking responsibility for our work that it does not occur to us to talk to God about it. It is so easy to forget that Jesus admonishes us to depend on him constantly: to 'change and become like little children'. (Matt 18:3)

And there is the problem of pride. Some of us imagine that we can tackle any task quite competently without God's help so why talk to him about it? Yet another reason is that we fall into the trap of believing that God would not be interested in the mundane matters which fill most hours of many days; that he has more important things to think about than the frustrations and choices which perplex and pressurise us. Then there is the problem of wilful disobedience – those times when we know we have failed God so, like Adam and Eve, we hide from him instead of drawing near to him.

Sometimes, too, when life feels full of frustrations, disppointments and difficulties, Paul's claim that God has blessed us with 'every spiritual blessing in Christ', (Eph 1:3) seems to have a hollow ring about it. Few of us have reached the stature of Job who could say: 'Though he slay me yet will I hope in him.' (Job 13:15) Conversely, when things are going well and we are happy, we are tempted to forget that the source of all true happiness is God. One person admitted to me that she used to try to talk to and consult God about the minutiae of life but she had been rebuked by other Christians who had convinced her that this was not an authentic way of praying. This is tragic because, as another young Christian testified, when we remember Brother Lawrence's advice and act on it, we, too can say:

> The God of the universe, the mighty One who made us and saves us, wants us to live in loving communion with His presence ... Every ordinary moment carries the possibility of awareness and encounter so deep and close it is like sitting down to share an intimate meal with [Him].[6]

Or, as this young man put it, 'I tell him that I love him and right there, in the middle of the chores, he tells me that he loves me back.'

It is for this reason that, in my *Prayer Journal*,[7] I have a section in which I record the requests I want to make of God. I approach this section by anticipating, as far as it is humanly possible to do so, the coming twenty-four hours. As the coming day flashes across my mind, I attempt to discern what I will need from God during those hours. And I write down my requests, leaving, in a parallel column, a space in which to record how he answered my prayer. Time and time again, I have been amazed by the specific ways in which he has attended to the details of my life. As Catherine Marshall observed, this practice is a great faith booster.

The young mum I mentioned in the first chapter of this book not only kept a diary but she, too, gained strength as she spread before God very ordinary requests. On the night the two little foster girls arrived she wrote: 'Lord, help us to see beyond the smell and dirt . . . give us the love we need to help them to settle quickly . . . Please give us wisdom and sensitivity that we may aid the bonding between the five children.'

Pray while you work

A few days later she wrote:

> Father, disciplining these children is very difficult. They've been locked away, physically and sexually abused, deprived of food and clothing. Please show us the way to show them right from wrong . . . I've still got the ironing to do, the pile seems bottomless.

This is the kind of prayer Brother Lawrence would encourage us to pray. This young mum not only prayed when faced with a challenge, she also prayed while she worked.

The retreat cook I mentioned told me that she did the same. So on the day when the dish-washer failed, the telephone went dead and the car refused to start, she still found herself held in the peace which was pervading every part of her being as she meditated and prayed. 'I talk to the Lord about all these things,' she said 'and I know that he is there helping me.'

Brother Lawrence also encouraged his retreatants

to pray in the middle of the maelstrom. He confessed that, at such times, he simply prayed a prayer like: 'Lord, I cannot do this unless you enable me.'[8]

Down the centuries, countless Christians have testified to the difference such prayer makes to the pressures they face. When they pray, instead of becoming knotted up, like Martha (Luke 10:40), they expect to see evidence of God's presence in their work place.

I think, for example, of Jackie Pullinger, a young woman whose prolonged presence among the poor and the drug addicts of Hong Kong earned her an MBE. In *Crack in the Wall*, she describes how, at first, she was beseiged by a sense of helplessness when faced with the stench and corruption of the Walled City – a particularly sordid part of Hong Kong. The surrounding tenements, the twelve-year-old prostitutes, the thousands of poor forced to live in one-room dwellings, the gangs and the opium dens both distressed her and drew from her a compassion which reflected the compassion of Christ and gave birth to a question: How could she even begin to pray for the inhabitants of this place? At first she felt defeated:

> Then I learned that praying in tongues was to help people when they did not know how to pray or had run out of words. Desperate by this time to see evidence of God's power in action I began to pray privately in tongues for the dying in the Walled City.
>
> After about six weeks I noticed a difference . . . Extraordinary things began to happen. A gangster fell to his knees in the streets, acknowledging Jesus and weeping. Another,

who had been badly beaten up, was miraculously healed. A young boy . . . gave up an organised gambling business. Praying in tongues was making me more sensitive to what the Holy Spirit was doing.

Soon I lost count of the number of changed lives around me.[9]

Praying in tongues is a devotional prayer language in-breathed by God's Spirit which people of prayer down the centuries have used. We witness the disciples praying in this way on the Day of Pentecost. Theresa of Avila prayed in tongues. So did Francis of Assisi, Florence Nightingale, John Wesley and many of history's unsung heroes and heroines.

The Jesus Prayer

But praying in tongues is not the only way to pray while we work. Another method is to pray the Jesus Prayer: a deceptively simple yet peculiarly powerful prayer which has been valued and prayed by innumerable members of the Orthodox Church down the centuries. The full prayer consists of the words, 'Lord Jesus Christ, Son of God, have mercy on me, a sinner', but it is often shortened to: 'Lord Jesus Christ, have mercy', 'Lord Jesus', or simply 'Jesus'.

'Jesus'. That is the key word and the power of the prayer lies in this name which is above every other name. As the hymn-writer expressed it:

Jesus, the name high over all
In heaven or earth or sky

Angels and men before it fall
And devils fear and fly.

Jesus the name that calms our fears
And bids our sorrow cease
'Tis music in the sinners ears
And life and health and peace.[10]

I use the abbreviated version of this prayer as I
turn from the busyness and attempt to enter the
grand silence of God. As I breathe in, I whisper the
beginning of the name: 'Je' and as I breathe out,
I complete the name: 'sus'. Praying in this way, I
find, brings me back to that still point where God is
most easily met and where his voice is most clearly
heard. I do not use the Saviour's name lightly or
as a mantra but rather as I might gently call a
friend's name if I was entering their house – just
to announce my arrival and to assure them that I
am present to them.

Increasingly, as I pray the prayer in this way, I
find it rising from my heart like a well-spring –
as I work, as I fall asleep, when I wake. Like the
pendulum of a grand-father clock, it reminds me
what the pace of my life should be. Like gravitational
pull, it draws me from a spinning-top life-style into
deep-down, hushed stillness. When I am walking, I
slow down so that the rhythm of my footsteps keeps
time with the rhythm of the full version of the prayer;
when I am resting or sitting at my desk, the prayer
seems to rock inside me like the gentle movement of
a boat or a rocking chair.

This prayer is particularly powerful because it can
be prayed at any time, no matter what we are doing.
A friend of mine, a widower, taught me this when

I visited him on one occasion. When I asked him how he was, a cloud passed over his face as he admitted that he was in turmoil because he had an important choice to make by the next morning. But then his eyes twinkled as he showed me a bowl of gooseberries and a panful of peas: 'I've had a wonderful afternoon,' he went on. 'First I topped and tailed the gooseberries and then I shelled the peas and all the while I was praying the Jesus Prayer: 'Lord Jesus Christ, Son of God, have mercy on me and guide me.'

Kallistos Ware in *The Power of the Name*, points out that the joy of the Jesus Prayer is that it may be said, once or many times, in the scattered moments which otherwise would be spiritually wasted: when occupied with some familiar and semi-automatic task, such as dressing, washing up, mending socks, or digging in the garden; when walking or driving, when waiting in a bus queue or a traffic jam; in a moment of quiet before some especially painful or difficult interview; when unable to sleep or before we have gained full consciousness on waking. Part of the distinctive value of the Jesus Prayer lies precisely in the fact that, because of its radical simplicity, it can be prayed in conditions of distraction when more complex forms of prayer are impossible. It is especially helpful in moments of tension and grave anxiety.[11]

I find that I can even pray this prayer while I am ploughing through a pile of paperwork or engrossed in a piece of creative writing. While concentrating on the task in hand, the prayer continues to sway inside me giving rise, very often, to a sense that

God is with me – so close that I sometimes sense him by my side.

The Jesus Prayer also makes a marvellous springboard for the prayer of gratitude. I discovered this one day as I was preparing vegetables for supper. For two days life had left me tempest-tossed and battered but as I lifted the situation to God, a shaft of light seemed to pierce the darkness. Suddenly I saw both the reason for the turmoil and a way out of it. Quite spontaneously, I found myself cutting courgettes and repeating: 'Lord Jesus Christ, Son of God, thank you for having mercy.'

Different people are discovering different ways of praying while they work. I think of the housewife I once stayed with who admits that she hates getting up in the morning. To make life possible for herself at the beginning of the day, she listens to quiet worship tapes as she prepares breakfast and I recall with gratitude the sense of calm which permeated her kitchen when I emerged from my room to share breakfast with her.

Or I think of the woman I read about who summarises each Sunday's sermon in writing and attaches her precis to her fridge. Every time she uses the fridge she is reminded of insights which now wait to be translated into life.

And I recall a personal discovery I made while I was convalescing from major surgery on one occasion. My brain seemed to be as anaesthetised as my body had been. None of my normal prayer practices worked. But I found a method of prayer commonly called mindfulness kept me in close touch with God.

Unable to concentrate on reading or writing, I decided that I would tackle some simple, practical

tasks which could be completed quite quickly and which would therefore give me a sense of fulfilment when they were completed. I would start by cleaning the kitchen cupboards. The prayer of mindfulness begins here – by choosing a chore which clamours for attention. It can be non-cerebral like 'washing-up, cleaning a bicycle, washing a car, weeding, raking, dusting, polishing – anything like that'.[12] Equally, it can be demanding, creative or fulfilling tasks: writing letters, writing essays, articles or sermons, answering the telephone or coping with administrative tasks.

I decided to heed the advice of those more skilled in this kind of prayer than I am:

Make a deliberate decision to do the chore and

that alone ... Do the task ... slowly, carefully and in silence. It doesn't matter that there will be noise and movement around you, just do it silently and calmly. If the task is the kind which requires little or no thought, as you work, concentrate on the physical feeling of what you're doing – the sensation in your hands, arms, legs, feet, body, neck and head. Become aware of the smells and sounds around you as you work.[13]

Time and time again, I found that the claims which are made of this kind of prayer are accurate: 'Gradually you will find your silence becoming inner stillness, a state of peace in which you will be more aware of God's encircling presence.'[14]

And I was deeply moved that, in doing ordinary things with extraordinary concentration and attention, I encountered God, there in my own kitchen.

Some white-collar workers protest that, while this method of prayer might work for those faced with practical, manual tasks, it would not work for them. My own experience and that of others persuades me to dispute this assumption. Just as, while I am working at my desk, the Jesus Prayer continues to 'rock' in my innermost being so, while I work, it frequently seems as though the Risen Lord hovers by my side smiling on me and assuring me of his presence and love.

A friend of mine experiences a similar sense of God's presence. Since she is a vicar's wife who is often called to the telephone, she has written herself a note and stuck it to the phone. It reads: 'Pray ... before, during and after ...'

Brother Lawrence would have applauded that note. He encourages us to turn to God, not simply before we work and while we work but, when the task is finished, to reflect with God on what we have done. He told the Abbot that when his own prayerful post-mortem exposed failure of any kind he would do nothing else but confess his shortcomings and say to God: 'I shall always fail if you leave me to myself; hinder my falling and mend whatever is missing in my life.'[15] After that he gave his fault no further thought.

On another occasion, he admitted that he had learned to be quite philosophical about his short-comings, admitting: 'When I feel convicted of a fault I do not deny it and I say: That is the way with me. That is all I do..' Without anxiety or feeling the need to grovel, he would confess and expect to receive 'the pardon which comes from the Blood of Jesus Christ'.[16] And he would return to his life's goal – seeking to express his love for God with his thoughts, words and actions.

This particular pen portrait of the famous monk reminds me of the small boy who, while playing with a friend, accidentally spilled paint on the back porch of his house.

"What will your father say?" asked his frightened playmate.

"Oh, he'll understand," came the boy's confident reply.

And he was right. His father did understand and readily forgave him.

But Brother Lawrence's review of his day frequently exposed, not failure, but faithfulness. When he was aware of success in his life, he gave 'due thanks to God' and rejoiced at this evidence that God was gradually transforming him.

And this picture of the humble, grateful monk

reminds me again of the girl I mentioned before – who was both a cook and a retreatant. On the day after the dish-washer died and while the car and telephone were still out of action, I asked her how she was feeling. Her face lit up and she replied: 'Joyce! God was so good to me yesterday,' and she described the ways in which God had so clearly intervened and turned what might have been a dismal day into a joyful one. Like Brother Lawrence, her impression of God as Love is so strong that she is well able to enter to the full into the celebration of busyness I mentioned at the end of the introduction to this book. She refuses to grow discouraged when faced with difficulties and personal failure; she seeks God's help with the tasks which fill her day, she prays while she works as well as before and after the day's duties.

Like Brother Lawrence, she shows us how to pray our life. I would love to introduce her to the social worker and the young mum, the commuter and the nurses with whom I began this book. In that she showed me how busyness can shape our attitude, she has been my teacher.

For personal reflection

1. What makes it easy for you to seek God's help when beginning a new day or project? What makes it difficult?

2. Resolve to make a conscious effort to practice God's presence, that is, to tune into an awareness of his love no matter how busy your day is. Give yourself an appraisal from time to time, not so that you can either gloat or grovel but to help you draw more fully on God's grace.

3. Spend some time practising the prayer of mindfulness which I describe in chapter 3.

4. If you have the gift of tongues, use it while you work and walk as well as in your times of stillness.

5. Practise praying your version of the Jesus Prayer.

6. Remember to 'pray as you can, not as you can't. In other words, if a particular method of prayer helps you draw near to God, use it. If it does not help, leave it on one side for now and come back to it on a future occasion.

CHAPTER 4

PULLING INTO LIFE'S LAY-BYS

I had just finished writing chapter 3 when a letter arrived from one of the doctors I mentioned at the beginning of this book. She has recently gone to work in a part of the world where the poverty and deprivation are horrifying:

Work is very difficult . . . I feel so much pain for these children and their very poor families . . . There is frustration knowing what could be done with a little more money or a few more people to help. I suppose it's an old story, but it's all new to me . . .

I go through the day one patient at a time, trying not to fret about the previous one nor wonder what mysterious ailment the next one will have . . . How do I begin to be still before the Lord? He is answering that one for me . . . I don't have to be alone in a quiet place. It's there waiting for me in a few still moments such as when I look into a child's peaceful eyes or look out at the storm in the afternoon. I *must* be obedient to him by being still enough inwardly that I can hear his voice when he speaks. Sometimes that's in the middle of a chaotic, exhausting day. I find that he is present at all times, and that in the worst moments at the hospital I am being made aware of his presence.

I read that letter many, many times – partly because I was moved by the doctor's testimony, partly because the letter was evidence of God's grace and partly because it pin-points so many of Brother Lawrence's principles and practical suggestions.

Seek life's little lay-bys

He encourages us, for example, to seek the little lay-bys or 'Kingdom moments' which can be found if we look at our day creatively:

When we are busied ... we ought to cease for one brief moment, as often as we can, to worship God in the depth of our being, to taste Him though it be in passing, to touch Him as it were by stealth. Since you cannot but know that God is with you in all you undertake, that He is at the very depth and centre of your soul, why should you not thus pause an instant from time to time in your outward business, and even in the act of prayer, to worship Him within your soul, to praise Him, to entreat His aid, to offer Him the service of your heart, and give Him thanks for all His loving-kindnesses and tender mercies.

What offering is there more acceptable to God than thus throughout the day to quit the things of outward sense, and to withdraw to worship Him within the secret places of the soul. In very truth we can render to God no greater or more signal proofs of our trust and faithfulness, than by this turning from things created, to find our joy, though for a single moment, in the Creator ... I am confident it is a common error among religious persons to neglect this practice of ceasing for a time that which they are engaged upon to worship God in the depth of their soul and to enjoy the peace of brief communion with him.[1]

'The common error' he mentions is as familiar today as it was when Brother Lawrence made this observation. So teachers of prayer continue to stress the value and need of life's 'little pools of silence'. Like Catherine de Hueck Doherty who insists in *Poustinia* that:

If we are to witness to Christ in today's market-place where there are constant demands on our whole person, we need silence. If we are to be always available, not only physically, but by empathy, sympathy, friendship, understanding and boundless *caritas* [love], we need silence. To be able to give joyous, unflagging hospitality, not only of house and food, but of mind, heart, body and soul, we need silence.[2]

Such silence is a state of mind and heart. It 'can be found in the midst of the city, and in the every day of our lives'.[3] It will come as we recognise our tremendous need for it and search for it:

These 'little solitudes' are often right behind a door which we can open, or in a little corner where we can stop to look at a tree that

somehow survived the snow and dust of a city street. There is the solitude of a car in which we return from work, riding bumper to bumper on a crowded highway.[4]

Or

Consider the solitude of walking from the subway train or bus to your home in the evening, when the streets are quieter and there are few passersby. Consider the solitude that greets you when you enter your room to change your office or working clothes to more comfortable, homey ones. Consider the solitude of a housewife, alone in the kitchen, sitting down for a cup of coffee before beginning the work of the day. Think of the solitudes afforded by such humble tasks as housecleaning, ironing, sewing . . .[5]

Sue Monk Kidd says something similar:

We can create special places where we are solitary for a while. A seat in the garden, a special chair in the den, a window seat. There we can peel away everything but God alone, even if it is only for three or four minutes. Or we can use the office desk at noon, when everyone else has gone to lunch, or early in the morning before others get there . . . God is constantly and abundantly available.[6]

The Bible assures us that when we pull into these welcome lay-bys we can be certain that God is already there to greet us. As Paul puts it: 'God is actually not far from any one of us.' (Acts 17:27, GNB) Or as James expresses it: 'Come near to God, and he will come near to you.' (James 4:8) And, of course, Jesus himself promised: 'I will not leave you as orphans, I will come to you.' (John 14:18)

Jesus not only promised his presence, he, himself frequently pulled out of the fast lane and into a lay-by. Like the young doctor who wrote to me and like most others who live in the fast lane, Jesus had no *one* place where he could steal away for much-needed rest. He did not even have a home to call his own: 'Foxes have holes and birds of the air have nests, but the Son of Man has nowhere to lay his head.' (Matt 8:20)

Instead, he learned to be creative: to enter into his Father's presence anywhere and everywhere. The exact venue did not matter because his real prayer place was portable. He encountered his Father in his own heart – the Bible's word for the well-spring of our lives – the innermost recesses of our being.

Because thoughts of God were never far from his mind, very ordinary objects and situations became sign-posts pointing to the existence and presence of God: flowers, grass and clover, sparrows and vines, sheep and goats, yeast and bread, fish and snakes, children at play, women endlessly sweeping their houses, pearls, farmers, fishermen.

I sometimes gaze at the exotic flowers which grow wild in Cyprus where I now live, and sense the reason why, for Jesus, wild flowers triggered off a paean of praise as they reminded him of the abundance and lavishness of his Father's provision and love: 'See how the lilies of the field grow. They do not labour or spin. Yet I tell you that not even Solomon in all his splendour was dressed like one of these. If that is how God clothes the grass of the field . . . will he not much more clothe you?' (Matt 6:28-30)

Or, as I walk in the vineyards towards the sea,

watching and listening for the tell-tale rustle in the grass which betrays the presence of a snake, again I sense I hear him thinking of his Father.

> Which of you, if his son asks for bread, will give him a stone? Or if he asks for a fish, will give him a snake? If you, then, though you are evil, know how to give good gifts to your children, how much more will your Father in heaven give good gifts to those who ask him! (Matt 7:9-11)

In Jesus, we see the truth of Teilhard de Chardin's claim: 'God . . . is not far away from us . . . Rather He awaits us every instant in our action, in the work of the moment . . . He is at the tip of my pen, my brush, my needle – of my heart and of my thought.'[7]

Discover the lay-by within

God is at the tip of our hearts and of our thoughts. He is Immanuel, God with us. For, according to Paul, we also possess a portable prayer place into which we may retreat at any time and in any place: We ourselves are 'living temples of the living God.' (1 Cor 6:19 J.B.Phillips)

In similar vein Brother Lawrence claims:

> It is not needful always to be in church to be with God. We can make a chapel of our heart, to which we can from time to time withdraw to have gentle, humble, loving communion with him. Everyone is able to have these familiar conversations with God, some more, some less – he knows our capabilities.[8]

God is everywhere, in all places, and there is no spot where we cannot draw near to Him, and hear Him speaking in our heart; with a little *love* just a very little, we shall not find it hard.[9]

In other words, the lay-by we need so urgently can be found, not simply in a quiet place, but in the middle of noise, chaos and busyness because we possess, deep inside us, a rest-place of the heart. When we have learned to retreat into this secret oasis, we shall find that, like Jesus, everything will trigger a prayer. Beauty will prompt us to praise whereas the distress we feel as we see and hear and read about the homeless, the starving, the destitute, the abused, the sick, the dying, the bereaved and others in need will draw from us the prayer of intercession and the desire to alleviate some of this suffering.

We shall also discover the joy, the pain and the privilege of becoming 'Christ-bearers', to borrow Catherine de Hueck Doherty's phrase:

Suppose that you were married and became pregnant. Would you stop cooking for your husband? Would you stop doing the laundry, the cleaning, stop going to meetings on racial justice and school affairs? No. You'd go about your daily business. The only difference between you and everyone else would be that you were carrying a child . . .

Wherever you go you are pregnant with Christ, and you bring his presence as you would bring the presence of a natural child . . . Applying this example to the mystery of being pregnant with God (and it applies to both men and women) . . . it is as if within you there was a little log cabin in which you and Christ are very close; in this attitude you go about your business . . . You bring [God] to the street, the party, the meeting, in a very special and powerful way . . . You are pregnant with Christ. You are Christ-bearers.[10]

As we move into the maelstrom, carrying our secret, the indwelling Christ, conscious that we are Christ-bearers, we find ourselves wanting to work from a healed and harmonious centre rather than from a harrassed and hurting heart. Then the avalanche of paperwork on our desk, the telephone which rings incessantly, the queue of patients in the waiting room, or our own form of pressure draws from us the desire to be contemplative in action as well as active in contemplation. As Brother Lawrence puts it: 'We must do all that we do with thoughtfulness and consideration, without impetuosity of haste, both of which show an undisciplined spirit; we must work quietly, placidly and lovingly before God, and pray to him to approve the work of our hands.'[11]

Do everything for him

When we become conscious that we are Christ-bearers, like Brother Lawrence, we shall want to do everything *for* God. He himself could claim that, when he tossed a pancake or picked up a piece of straw from the ground, he did it for the King.

A refugee worker once helped me to understand what this involves. She had just returned from Iraq where she had been engaged in relief work among

Kurdish refugees whom she had grown to love. Now she was attending a retreat and I had the privilege of being her prayer guide.

One morning I suggested that, for her meditation, she should read the story of the Good Samaritan and project herself into the narrative by assuming the role of the rescuer – the good Samaritan himself; that she should imagine that the man stripped by robbers was one of the Kurdish children she had been trying to help.

Next day she told me what had happened as she stepped into this parable. As she travelled, in her imagination, along the Jerusalem to Jericho road, she saw the Priest and the Levite pass by the naked, helpless body slumped by the side of the road. But she couldn't do that. Assuming the baby to be a Kurdish child, she went to the rescue. Being a nurse, as she came closer to the little girl, she prepared herself to wash the wounds, feed the child, then carry her to a sheltered place. But as she stooped over the body, she gasped. It was not a Kurdish refugee, it was Jesus. She went to him, washed his wounds, gave him water and struggled to carry him to safety.

As her story unfolded, the words of Jesus rang in my ears:

When, Lord, did we ever see you hungry and feed you, or thirsty and give you a drink? When did we ever see you a stranger and welcome you in our homes, or naked and clothe you? When did we ever see you sick or in prison, and visit you? The King will reply, "I tell you, whenever you did this for one of the least important of these brothers of mine, you did it for me" (Matt 25:37-40, GNB)

'You did it for me!' For the nurse, too, it was a moment of revelation as she saw with a recognition she had not enjoyed previously, that in sacrificing so much to help, in a hidden way, the hungry and helpless, the broken-hearted and the dying, she had been pouring healing love into the wounds of Christ; she had been working for him.

Brother Lawrence urges us to adopt this attitude so that it colours everything we do. It is the attitude George Herbert sums up in his famous, though quaint, hymn:

Teach me my God and King
In all things Thee to see
That what I do in anything
To do it as for Thee.

A servant with this clause
Makes drudgery divine
Who sweeps a room as for Thy laws
Makes that and the action fine.[12]

Sue Monk Kidd, testifying to the joy of offering each new task to God 'whether it is typing a letter, giving a seminar or preparing a meal' adds: 'When I clean my sink for God, it sparkles and I take pleasure in Him as I work. When I clean the sink for myself, I grumble, cut corners and experience the work as drudgery.'[13]

The lay-by of love

Like Brother Lawrence, the prayer she suggests we pray at the beginning of each new endeavour is short and simple: 'I do this for you.' Brother Lawrence goes further as he emphasises that often the practice of the presence of God will be wordless. The presence of God, he claimed, is reached by the heart rather than the mind: 'In the way of God *thoughts* count for little, *love* is everything'[14], 'a little lifting up of the heart'; 'the least little remembrance', or even the occasional loving glance is sufficient.

I was attending a conference while I was thinking about this aspect of Brother Lawrence's teaching. I knew none of the people there but one coffee break my attention was attracted by two young people: a man and a woman. They were simply chatting, showing none of the usual signs that they were 'in love' but as the coffee break ended, a glance passed between them which conveyed mutual affection and admiration and which told me that they were more than just good friends. The loving look lasted less than a second but I had little doubt that, as lovers do, throughout the lengthy seminar which followed they would each be feasting on the adoration it silently and surreptitiously conveyed.

This is the kind of loving glance Brother Lawrence suggests we give to God and receive from him. It need scarcely interrupt what we are doing but it will be enough to strengthen us for the next little lap of the journey.

For some people, such loving glances are occasional and spontaneous. Others plan them: when the clock strikes, when they take a coffee or a lunch break, when they place a clean piece of paper into the type-writer or make a new file on the computer or start to read a fresh page of a book or magazine, or pick up the newspaper. Brother Lawrence stresses that these glances assume particular importance in the teeth of temptation when Satan seeks to side-track us from those long-term goals we considered in chapter 2; when he attempts to beguile us into believing that happiness may be found in the pursuit of pleasure and prestige, power and possessions. At such times, life's little lay-bys are life-savers. We may have time to withdraw into them only momentarily, but it will be long enough to remind ourselves of our life's goal and of the fact that the secret of our identity lies neither in pleasure, prestige nor possessions but rather within the love of the God to whom we have dedicated all we have and are.

Dryness and distress

If life's lay-bys assume particular importance in times of temptation when the 'sights that dazzle' and the tempting sounds seem so much more attractive than the ways of God, it is even more essential to pull out of the fast lane during those times of dryness which plague most Christians from time to time. The Psalmist powerfully describes these periods of aridity, emptiness or deadness when God seems more absent than present: 'How much longer will you forget me, Lord? For ever? How much longer will you hide yourself from me?' (Psalm 13:1, GNB)

Although such times take on the appearance of a spiritual desert where God seems to be both distant and silent, we should seek to rest with him in the lay-by because, with the wisdom of hindsight, we shall see that he has not deserted us as we might have been tempted to believe. Rather he has been there all the time, loving us in ways which remain hidden at the time.

This has been beautifully summed up in the anony-mous meditation commonly called 'Footprints'. Al-though this is now so well known and loved that it appears on post-cards and posters, lapel badges and plaques, I reproduce it here:

One night a man had a dream. He dreamed he was walking along the beach with the Lord. Across the sky flashed scenes from his life. For each scene he noticed two sets of footprints in the sand. One belonged to him and the other to the Lord. When the last scene of his life flashed before him, he looked back at the footprints in the sand. He noticed that many times along the path of his life there was only one set of footprints. He also noticed that it happened at the very lowest and saddest times in his life. This really bothered him and he questioned the Lord about it. 'Lord, you said that once I decided to follow you, you would walk with me all the way. But I have noticed that during the most troublesome times in my life, there is only one set of footprints. I do not understand why, when I needed you most, you would leave me.' The Lord replied, 'My precious child! I love you and would never leave you. During your times of trial and suffering, when you see only one set of footprints, it was then that I carried you.'[15]

If we believe that God will never abandon us, even when prayer produces little or no nourishment and our desire for him has dwindled to a puddle, we can continue to reach out to him, praying with the Psalmist:

As a deer longs for a stream of cool water,
   so I long for you, O God.
I thirst for you, the living God;
   when can I go and worship in your
     presence? . . .
My heart breaks when I remember the past,
   when I went with the crowds to the house
    of God
and led them as they walked along,
   a happy crowd, singing and shouting
   praise to God.
Why am I so sad?
   Why am I so troubled?
I will put my hope in God,
   and once again I will praise him,
   my saviour and my God. (Psalm 42:1-5, GNB)

When the time is ripe, God will make his presence known once more. His return will be as timely and creative as the farmer I have been watching on

the walk I enjoy most days. First he harvested his bumper crop of water melons. Next he ploughed the hard earth, turning it into a field full of furrows. For a while, he left the field fallow.

When he sensed the time was ripe, he returned and rigged up an impressive irrigation system connected to an artesian well. Although no rain fell, this field was no longer abandoned to the mercies of the summer sun. Water flowed along the furrows, new crops appeared like a green haze hovering over the rich-brown earth and the seeming desert was transformed, almost overnight, into arable land.

Brother Lawrence has given us an irrigation system for our souls. By making use of life's lay-bys, doing everything contemplatively and for God and turning to him in times of temptation and turbulence, the parched places of our lives may blossom and grow like well-tended, well-watered fields and we shall be able to testify, with the writer of Deuteronomy:

In a desert land he found [me],
   in a barren and howling waste.
He shielded [me] and cared for [me];
   he guarded [me] as the apple of his eye.
   (Deut.32:10)

For personal reflection

1. Read the following meditation and if you find yourself reflected there, ask God to deliver you from the tyranny of the urgent:

Where is my peace?

Noise

> Telephones jangling: answer me, answer me!
> Doorbells ringing: hurry up, I have other places to go!
> Car radios blaring on street corners: look at me!
> Diners shouting: this is our space too!

Expectations

> You're just the one to do this job, Jim,
> We know you like to write so . . .
> When are you coming to see me?
> I know you're busy, but . . .
> This one is really important!

Interruptions

> I was just in town, and . . .
> Sorry to bother you, but I think we have a problem.
> I hate to call you at home . . .
> I don't mean to keep bugging you about this . . .

Myself

> Yes, God , it's a sound-polluted world. People demand more than I have to give. My broken

agendas litter the landscape of my existence. But I am the one who says yes in order to please. I am the one who fails to use chance moments to breathe in your grace and let go. I decide the schedule is too full to take my walk. I fail to plan a time apart to let you re-order my priorities. Help me, God, to make more prayerful choices. Bring your restoring peace to my waiting soul.[16]

2. Begin to establish for yourself a realistic rhythm by asking:
    – When and where can I be still most days?
    – Could I carve out extra time most months? If so, when? Where would I go? Put the dates in your diary now and make arrangements to go to a quiet place.
    – Could you go on retreat annually? Begin to make enquiries now.

3. What, for you, would constitute some of life's little lay-bys? Could you snatch some life-saving Kingdom moments there? Ask for the grace to seek such times and places and to use them to the full.

4. Ask, too, for the grace to recognise that ordinary things can be signposts which point to God. So, as you enjoy one of life's 'little solitudes', gaze at the things which lie before you: a flower maybe, a bird taking a bath in a puddle on the pavement, the beauty of an autumn leaf. Learn to ask yourself the following questions as you gaze:
    – What is God saying through this little piece of his creation?

     – What is he saying *to me*?
     – If I were that flower or bird or leaf or . . . , how might I feel?
     – How do I find myself responding to my Creator as I listen to the language spoken by the the work of his hands?

5.   Practice recollecting at the beginning of each new day that you move into the day as a Christ-bearer. Then review your day asking yourself where that awareness has helped to shape your attitudes, behaviour and life-style and where it has failed to make an impact. Talk to God about your discoveries.

6.   Think of a typical day in your week. Which things are you able to do 'for God'? Are there things you find difficult to do 'for him'? If so, ask yourself why you find it difficult to envisage your self serving *Christ* in this way.

CHAPTER 5

PACING YOURSELF

Whenever I list Brother Lawrence's prerequisites for practising the presence of God, I am amazed by their simplicity and ordinariness and wonder why I still struggle to observe them. I lamented my inexpertise to a friend on one occasion and his response helped me to recognise that, if we are serious about mastering this method of prayer, we must cultivate a conducive climate and pace ourselves accordingly. 'Remember that Brother Lawrence was a contemplative monk,' my mentor cautioned. The importance of that very obvious observation came with the force of a revelation when I was planning this chapter. Then, as I thought about the steps in the mountain path I described in chapter 3, I realised that there is a sense in which Brother Lawrence, as a Carmelite monk, started the upward climb from a vantage point which is denied to most Christians.

Thomas Merton outlines the advantages of the monastic life: 'The order, the quiet, the fraternal communication and love provided by a working and praying community are the obvious and ordinary place in which the life of prayer develops.'[1]

As we observed in chapter 1, Brother Lawrence's day would have begun in the early hours of the morning with a service in chapel where, with his fellow monks, he would have recalled the resurrection of Jesus and celebrated the gifts of life and the new day.

Breakfast, like all meals, would have been taken in silence and time would have been ear-marked for slow reading of the Scriptures, leisurely private prayer in the hushed chapel and other meditative reading. Each day would also have included a celebration of the Eucharist. There he would have been nourished by the bread and wine, the richness of the Bible readings and liturgical prayers, and by the deep-down silence which creeps over a congregation who unite silently to contemplate the mystery of the death and resurrection, ascension and constant intercession of the Son of God; who, thus drawn into the quiet depths of God's love, beg him to ignite within themselves the flame of reciprocal love.

Work would have been punctuated by regular times of communal prayer and Brother Lawrence would have experienced the joy of a supportive fellowship which wept when he wept and rejoiced when he rejoiced. His day would have ended with the calming, plaintive chants of the service of Compline and that moving prayer: 'Be present, O merciful God, and protect us through the silent hours of this night, so that we who are wearied by the changes and chances of this fleeting world may rest upon your eternal changelessness.'[2]

From time to time, I have hidden in such communities to write. Every time I have done so, I have found that my writing flows from my prayer as I have dropped, with gratitude, into the full but balanced monastic rhythm of life.

I once lived in silence with a group of nine others for five weeks. We ate in silence, washed up in silence and met for daily intercessions in silence. During the mainly-silent Eucharist, we seemed to hang on every word of the Bible readings and the prayers. On a few occasions it became necessary for me to make a foray into the nearby town. I would return with my mind in over-drive just as it often is when I work from home. But as soon as I returned to the Convent where we were staying, I would be drawn back into that still place where God's voice is most clearly heard and where life can be viewed from his perspective: that place where true worship is born.

Brother Lawrence admits in his letters that, in his early days as a monk, he spent a great deal of the prescribed stillness soaking up the love of God. He did this by meditating on the Scriptures – particularly the words of Jesus recorded in the Gospels, and through enjoying personal encounters with the God of love: from just 'being' rather than 'doing'. It was from this loved place that he emerged into his hectic kitchen.

Compare that renewing rhythm of life to the frenetic life-style most Christians attempt to live: those who start their day on noisy, over-crowded buses or by being jostled and jolted to work on London's Underground trains or those whose journey to work takes them through miles of diesel fumes and rush hour traffic. It then quickly becomes obvious that Brother Lawrence had a head start. This was underlined for me while I was writing this chapter. The screams of my neighbour's adorable but wilful child pierced the silence of my study; when the tantrums stopped the strident shouting, hammering and drilling of builders working on a neighbouring house shattered the silence once more, and people hurling questions which demanded instant answers by phone or fax seemed determined to wind me up rather than provide me with the space I needed to gather my thoughts.

I recalled that climb up the mountains I described in chapter 3 – when my husband and I discovered steps cut into the stony path. We cheated that day. It was hot so we drove our car for two kilometres along a very rough, tortuous track so that we could begin our climb as near as possible to the waterfall we hoped to find. Other climbers, however, had no car. Some walked the two kilometres and then started the steep ascent. Others turned back, unable to make the climb in the noon-day heat and never finding those helpful steps.

Brother Lawrence had a lift in a car, as it were, when he began to practice the presence of God. We who do not live in monasteries, on the other hand, are like the car-less climbers – doomed to make the steep ascent the hard way. We need to remember this if we are not to grow discouraged in our determination to practice the presence of God. We also need to beware of attempting the impossible: of practising the presence of God while persisting in a life-style which is designed to fragment rather than to heal, which revolves around self rather than around God, which is lived under the lordship of anyone or anything other than the Lord Jesus Christ. And this will mean, to change the metaphor back from climbing to driving, moving out of the fast lane and into a resting place at regular intervals.

Move out of the fast lane

Thomas Merton underlined the importance of this:

If we really want prayer, we'll have to give it time. We must slow down to a human tempo . . .

The reason why we don't take time is a feeling that we have to keep moving. This is a real sickness. Today, time is a commodity, and for each one of us time is mortgaged ... we must approach the whole idea of time in a new way.[3]

Merton spoke from the platform of his own struggles: 'What I needed was the solitude to expand in breadth and depth and to be simplified out under the gaze of God more or less the way a plant spreads out its leaves in the sun.'[4] His desire for solitude was experienced as a thirst which he believed we all experience. Few of us can embrace the solitude of a contemplative monk, but the need for some solitude is essential for all of us rather than a luxury.

Like Merton, Sue Monk Kidd claims that we need solitude not for perfection but for survival. 'It is a return to the centre. It is not something remote, something to be thought of later on, in the future, when I am not so busy, under so much pressure. It is now.'[5]

In *God's Joyful Surprise*, she contrasts life lived from this centre to life in the fast lane. Speaking from her own experience she testifies:

Mine was a divided life without a nourishing whole. And the disharmony of all the competing pieces, the desires and conflicts that pulled in every direction within, led to inner tensions which had actually become so intense they had created physical changes in my body. Chest pains and galloping pulse.[6]

The health crisis forced her to change her life-style

– to discover the life-saving solitude Thomas Merton advocates. Then she could write with integrity:

> We don't withdraw from the world to a center. We respond to the world from our center. Instead of rushing about, accepting every job that comes, we get a sense of what's really important. Being centred allows us to bring that elusive quality of focus to our lives. It enables us to set priorities. From the center we can respond to the chaos by eliminating that which isn't meaningful and bringing order and calm to the rest. For in the center we are rooted in God's love. In such a place there is no need for striving and impatience and dashing about seeking approval.[7]

We who sometimes sacrifice so much by living in the fast lane need to recognise that there are times to drive with the foot hard on the accelerator, times to pull into life's lay-bys and times to stop and seek real refreshment – from stillness and worship, meditation and fellowship with others, the Eucharist and many other forms of prayer. We need to pace ourselves so that, instead of driving ourselves relentlessly, hindered by unhealed hurts, burdened by bewilderment and other excess emotional baggage, functioning from a fearful and fragmented centre, we enjoy a harmony which embraces and celebrates busyness and stillness. Then, to change the image, our lives will resemble a giant cartwheel. Part of us (the rim) will keep in contact with the ground and keep in touch with the nitty gritty of the everyday and ordinary. At the same time we will recall that this outer rim is held together by many spokes which represent a variety of ways of praying which are essential for our survival and efficiency. These spokes unite at the hub where all is still and unpressurised.[8]

Establish a Realistic Rhythm

The only way to achieve this harmony is to establish for our selves a rhythm of life which frees us to operate from the hub rather than from the rim – to know ourselves well enough to discern the nature of this much-needed rhythm and then to plan well ahead so that we give ourselves the gift of times when our relationship with God can genuinely be renewed.

Most of us, for example, need daily times of solitude when we, too, can return to the hub, read the Scriptures slowly and meditatively, be nourished and guided by this 'letter from home'[9] and be drawn into the grand silence of God where we are reassured that we are uniquely and unconditionally loved by him. Making our way from the rim to the hub may require initiative, imagination and determination.

When I was a student sharing a room with an atheist, for example, such solitude could only be snatched in the bathroom of the hall of residence in the small hours of the morning. Many young mums find that the only time they can savour this silence is while they are breast-feeding their babies. And many commuters find the respite from living from the rim lies behind their newspaper in the train, the bus or the plane.

The most moving testimony I have ever heard was from a woman whose husband became violent whenever he suspected she was praying. When I asked her how she overcame this difficulty, she admitted that, since she and her husband spent most evenings watching television together, she had cultivated the art of finding inner stillness while the commercials were on. When she closed her eyes at that time of evening, her husband thought she was dozing but she was praying and reciting Scripture. And a businessman who has just written to me ends the letter scribbled in his lunch break with: 'I must go and take my "survival walk".' His lunch-time break harnesses exercise and much-needed time at the hub.

Plan ahead

In addition to such snatched times of stillness, most of us need opportunities when we can enjoy a more leisurely time away from the rim – a sustained experience of God's love. Increasingly, quiet places are being established where we can return to our centre. I have on my desk, for example, a card telling me of a newly-created prayer place:

> where you can enjoy undisturbed time with God, away from the busyness and pressures of daily living. It is a peaceful room offering comfort and warmth with facilities for prayer, sleep, reading, writing and for making drinks. You simply bring something to eat, unless you wish to stay overnight and be catered for. The room is available Mondays to Fridays. If required, a Spiritual Director is available for a one hour session. Prior booking is necessary. Donations are welcomed to cover the cost of providing the facility.[10]

I recently read of an elderly lady who has been making a room in her house available in this way for many years. She supplies visitors with coffee, a light lunch and tea and sees this as part of her ministry in her advancing years.

Many dioceses are sensing the need to establish 'quiet prayer places' in each deanery and I have been thrilled to visit some of these – particularly those which are being set up in cities where the wear and tear on people's whole person is considerable.[11]

For the past seventeen years, I have found it

helpful to adopt such a place as my spiritual home and to start the year by ear-marking in advance a day a month when I can go there to be quiet. Like Thomas Merton, I have found that this personal rhythm, though a far cry from the monastic calm Brother Lawrence enjoyed, is part of my survival kit. The busier I become, the more I enter into the abundance of life lived in God, the more I feel the need to move from a sense of being loved into a whirl of activity. These away days are therefore part of my spiritual life blood.

In Imitation of Jesus

'But isn't this selfish? Pure escapism?' people some-times protest when I suggest that they should estab-lish a rhythm for themselves. If we examine the example of Jesus, the quick answer to that question is a resounding: 'No!'

Of all people, Jesus' life resembles a well-maintained cartwheel. In fact, he flatly refused to live from the rim and planned his programme so that stillness and busyness were held together by a whole variety of spokes.

I think of the first chapter of Mark's Gospel, for example. Here Mark paints a powerful pen-picture of Jesus experiencing the wear and tear of life near the rim. We find him teaching in the synagogue and exercising the deliverance ministry on a demon-possessed man. Drained by these pieces of work, he appears to have been taken to Peter's home for lunch and the customary siesta, but there he finds, not the expected, much-needed refreshment, but a sick woman: Peter's feverish mother-in-law. He heals her. Sunset provides no respite, only a fresh round of demands: 'the whole town' clamour round the house begging to be touched by the miracle-worker.

The phrase 'the whole town' conjures up for me a picture of an uncontrollable crowd of gregarious, spontaneous people making no attempt to hide their emotions but rather chattering incessantly and noisily, weeping and wailing openly, pleading with Jesus to touch and heal the lame and the deaf, the blind and the dying who have been dragged by them to Peter's house. They would have syphoned all remaining energy from Jesus and he would have gone to bed as exhausted and drained as the most harassed commuter or the most pressurised social worker, nurse or young mum. Having spent the Sabbath pouring himself out for others, living from the rim, and feeling the pain of others, very early next morning, before the rising sun could turn the world from pearl to pink then set the sky and Sea of Galilee ablaze with glory, possibly while the moon still flooded the fields with its silver light, he creeps to a quiet place where he can spend time at the hub receiving a fresh inflow of his Father's life and love.

This was not the only occasion when he retreated in this way. It seems to have been a regular occurence. We read of him retiring often – to places where he could be renewed by his Father's love and where he could receive his Father's wisdom. In Matthew 14:23, for example, after Jesus had spent another hectic day teaching and healing the multitudes and while he was struggling to come to terms with his grief – having heard the news that his cousin, John the Baptist had been butchered to death by Herod

– we find him on the mountainside alone. Similarly, on the day before he called the Twelve to follow him, he went again to the mountainside where he spent the entire night under the velvet, star-studded sky. (Luke 6:12)

And on the night before he died, he retired to another of his prayer places, the Garden of Gethsemane, where he poured out his heart to his Father and received from him the grace, courage and strength to go to the gallows for us.

Just as the moon waxes and wanes and the sea ebbs and flows and just as nature sleeps before bursting with new life in Spring, so Jesus enjoyed the renewal which comes through living rhythmically.

So, no. To retreat is not selfish. It is vital for our effectiveness. I sometimes think of it in this way. When I make a long journey by car, I do not think it selfish to break my journey by enjoying a leisurely meal on the way. I plan such survival breaks in

advance. Pulling off the road in this way helps me to concentrate when I am driving and so aids safe travelling. Similarly, if we are wise, we build breaks into our busy schedules – for our sanity, survival and spiritual safety.

In my own times of quiet, I often turn to a little book called *I Am with You*. The book consists of a number of 'sayings' which John Woolley, Chaplain of Hill End Hospital, St Alban's, sensed God was asking him to record over a period of time. This one sums up the situation well:

My child, every moment which you set aside for Me has more than the obvious benefits for you. Not only are you receiving healing of the spirit and light for your way, but such occasions will affect the atmosphere of your busier moments, when perhaps, you are unable to focus fully upon Me.

Your deliberate making of time for our spirits to be in communion helps to enlarge My activity in your life, so that you become increasingly aware of My presence – even when there is much to pre-occupy you this awareness ensures the death of self.

It will be My Spirit in you which causes you to give that momentary glance in My direction when life is turbulent, and when you need, desperately, the steadiness which comes only from Me.

Feed your spirit, alone with Me, whenever you can, and let this communion with Me carry over into life's most demanding periods.

Wait upon Me, listen to Me, and your soul shall live. (Isaiah 55:3)[12]

Check that you are 'on course'

'It will be My Spirit in you which causes you to give that momentary glance in My direction when life is turbulent.' I suspect Brother Lawrence would have liked that sentence because, as we observed in chapter 1, he stresses our dependence on God's grace:

A soul is the more dependent on grace, the higher the perfection to which it aspires; and the grace of God is the more needful each moment, as without it the soul can do nothing. The world, the flesh, and the devil join forces and assault the soul so straitly and so untiringly that, without humble reliance on the ever-present aid of God, they drag the soul down in spite of all resistance. Thus to rely seems hard to nature, but grace makes it become easy, and brings with it joy.[13]

We need God's grace, not only to sustain us and enable us to turn to God in times of turbulence, we also need his grace to discern whether we are 'on course' or whether we have been side-tracked by those terrible triplets: 'the world, the flesh and the devil'.

I was thinking about this one evening while I was lying in bed reading. Out of the corner of my eye, I could see an insect crawling across my bed-side table. At first I thought it was an ant but closer examination revealed beautiful, blue markings on its body and transparent wings. I was still watching it, marvelling at its unique beauty, when suddenly it disappeared. It had fallen headlong over the back of the table but as I peered into the semi-darkness,

I noticed it had not fallen to the floor but into the clutches of a spider which had been lurking in the centre of a web attached to the table-leg. Seized by the spider's long, amazingly-strong fingers, the small creature fought frantically but was clearly helpless. For its survival it was dependent on someone bigger and more powerful that itself to come to the rescue.

The devil monitors our progress as we travel along the path which leads to God and uses his allies, the world and the flesh to lure us up cul-de-sacs or even to stifle the spiritual life which motivates us to continue on the journey when the going is rough.

While we rush around like whirling dervishes, we fail to detect how successful his tactics are. That is another reason why we need to stop from time to time and to ask some probing questions like: Am I being beguiled by the world? Am I in control of my appetites and ambitions or are they controlling me?

In *I Believe in Satan's Downfall*, Michael Green defines 'the world' as a society which leaves God out of account and 'the flesh' as 'the seat of our lusts'.[14] The secular society in which we live has become the womb of consumerism. It gives birth to the belief that our value and identity may be monitored by the size of the pay-packet we bring home, the area of the country in which we live or the title or role our job gives us. These are false values. Our true identity is firmly rooted in God and in him alone. As Christians we need, therefore, to challenge these assumptions by regularly putting to ourselves another question: Am I being beguiled by the lies of the cultural climate in which I live?

Our secular society goes further. It manipulates us through advertising creating in us a terrible lust for things we neither need nor really want. The consequences are terrifying. Think, for example, of the effect this has on parents, to mention but one section of society. Although in the winter of 1992, England was held in the grip of a deep and devastating economic recession, it was estimated that parents of young children were preparing to spend £60 on each child's Christmas presents to satisfy their lusts. Instead of pointing the finger at this anomaly, we each need to ask ourselves another pertinent question: Am I being ensnared by the world's philosophy? Am I being swayed by the powerful tug of lust?

The materialistic world which leaves God out of its reckoning also assaults our ambitions, persuading us to serve self, to fight for our rights, to grab what we want even though our greed may eat into non-renewable resources endangering the livelihood of others. The result is escalating cosmic chaos. It is therefore vital that we embark on a spiritual check-up periodically asking: Whose Kingdom am I serving? The Kingdom of self or the Kingdom of God?

In addition to the influence of the secular society, our own appetites add to the problem. Appetites quickly become addictions. As Michael Green expresses it: 'The amount of evil that comes into the world through the misuse of perfectly natural bodily functions, the desire for food, drink, sex, sleep and strength is simply enormous.'[15]

And he does not mention many other appetites: for news and gossip, pleasure and possessions, prestige and power.

Again we ask the question: whose Kingdom am I serving? All is not doom and gloom, of course, because the Holy Trinity is more powerful than the terrible triplets. Jesus is greater than Satan, 'the prince of this world'. Jesus claims '[The devil, the Anti-Christ] has no power over me'. (John 14:30)

Jesus, therefore, is the One who can give us the grace to rebuke Satan as he himself did; to say to him: 'I refuse to be governed by my appetites and ambitions. My life is governed by God.' But unless we stop for long enough to discern Satan's ruses and to deal with them, we may find ourselves speeding along a diversion rather than straight along the road which leads to God.

Our arch-enemy is not powerless. 'He is set for our downfall, and will come at us either as the king of the jungle, the "roaring lion seeking whom he may devour" (1 Peter 5:8) or else seductively as the "angel of light" (2 Cor 11:14) seeking whom he may deceive.'[16] We must therefore be vigilant (1 Peter 5:8) – as watchful as I have been while writing this book. While I was writing the first draft in my garden one morning, I became aware of movement among the miniature roses. At first I thought it was a harmless lizard. Then my heart froze as I watched the shiny body of a big, black snake slither across the patio and into the vineyard beyond.

We need to be not only watchful, but receptive. The Holy Trinity: the Father, the Son and the Holy Spirit, add to us all the resources we need to combat the world, the flesh and the devil. This certainty rings like a peal of joyful bells through so many of Jesus' parables – like the parable of the Good Samaritan. A popular Egyptian writer likens us to the man who was mugged on the Jerusalem to Jericho road. He likens the thieves to Satan and the Good Samaritan to Jesus the One on whose grace we depend for every step of life's pilgrimage.[17]

Check your current image of God.

We will need every ounce of that grace when the world, the flesh and the devil challenge our belief and trust in God. Since Genesis Chapter 3, Satan has been attempting to sow in people's minds seeds of doubt about God's goodness, insisting that God is the great Depriver instead of the great Provider. Eve believed him and it sometimes surprises Christians to discover how easy it is to follow her example. Satan's suggestions are so subtle. Because we spend most of our time speeding along the fast lane, creating little quality time for God, we pine for him. Instead of admitting our need of his love, we give vent to our frustration and accuse him of not loving us or of not being there. Or worse, we fall into the trap of believing God to be a spoilsport or a tyrant, an ogre or a punitive policeman.

It is only when we stop that we realise that it is not God who has abandoned us but we who have neglected him while, all the time, he was been waiting to strengthen, guide and cherish us.

There are times, too, when we feel the pressure and pain of living near the rim. At such times, our heads may give credence to the fact that love is what God is while our hearts refute this head-knowledge. It takes time for such truths to trickle from our head into our heart. Often people find that it is when they pause that their innermost being catches up with their head and they find themselves feeding on and relishing God's love, allowing it to touch them where they hunger and hurt.

This is another reason why withdrawing to the hub, from time to time, is vital. As Brother Lawrence insists, if we are to find God at the interface with a turbulent world, it is essential that we do not lose sight of the unassailable fact of the innate goodness of God.

When problems persist, the need for resting places becomes even more pressing. There we can seek to make sense of what is happening to us or around us. There we have more chance of taking on board a further piece of the monk's advice:

If we were well disciplined in the practice of the presence of God, all bodily maladies would be light to us now. Often God allows us to suffer a little to purify our soul, and to compel us to abide with him . . . Offer him ceaselessly your sufferings. Beg him for strength to bear them . . . Forget him as little as you can. Worship him in your infirmities. Keep repeating your self-surrender.[18]

Many twentieth-century Western Christians find this pill hard to swallow. Deep down, we somehow believe that if we show our allegiance to Christ by praying, attending church and serving our neighbour, God owes us a quiet, crisis free life. But that is not what Jesus promised. He prophesied: 'In this world you will have trouble.' (John 16:33)

He goes on to assure us that, ultimately, he is in control. This assurance seems to have been the bottom line of Brother Lawrence's belief. Writing to the 'Reverend Mother' he affirms:

We have a God infinitely good, and who knows what we need . . . He will come in his good time, and when you least expect him. Hope in him more than ever. Thank him for the favours that he shows you, particularly for the strength and the patience he is giving you in your afflictions – an evident sign of the care he has for you. Be comforted therefore in him and thank him for everything.[19]

'He will come in his good time.' When he comes, he refreshes us so that, though we might yearn to linger in his presence, we find ourselves content to continue our journey, conscious that the great cartwheel we have been picturing constantly carries the chassis of our life ever God-wards. We are called to be pilgrims – people on the move. But we do not make the journey alone. God lives at the hub. Like an ever-present companion, comforter and counsellor, he accompanies us on our journey. According to Brother Lawrence, it is never too late to discover how to relate to him nor to find ways of ensuring that effective methods of prayer connect him to the busyness and the busyness to him:

Think often of God, day and night, in all your tasks, in all your religious duties, even in all your amusements. He is always at your side. Do not fail in fellowship with him. You would consider it discourteous to neglect a friend who visited you. Why abandon God and leave him alone? Do not then forget him. Thank him often. Worship him all the time. Live and die with him. That is a Christian's lovely task, in a word, our calling.[20]

For personal reflection

1. Ask yourself the probing questions which peppered the pages of chapter 5:
   – Am I being beguiled by the lies of a secular society?
   – Has my philosophy of life been formed by the cultural climate in which I live or by the example and teaching of Christ?
   – Whose Kingdom am I serving? The Kingdom of self or the Kingdom of God?
   – Am I in control of my appetites and ambitions or are some of them in danger of controlling me? Talk to God about that.
   – Which of these vie for first place in my life: pleasure, possessions, prestige, popularity, sexual fulfilment (legitimate or other), serving Christ? Talk to God about your priorities.

2. Look back to question 2 at the end of chapter 4 and read or recollect any resolutions you made in response to this question. Now ask yourself whether you acted on them. If so, has this borne fruit. If not, act on your resolutions now.

3. Think of the various caricatures of God described in chapter 5. Compare them with your own image of God. If you were to describe him to a friend at this moment in time, what words or pen-pictures would you use?

4. Ask yourself how you can live nearer the hub as well as 'on the rim'.

CHAPTER 6

FOOD FOR THE JOURNEY

Someone once confided in me: 'Ever since I became a Christian, people have been telling me I ought to pray for half an hour a day but what I want to know is how to pray my life, not how to fill up these half-hour God-slots.'

At the end of the last chapter, we noted Brother Lawrence's succinct solution to this problem: 'Live and die with him.' In other words, encounter God at all times. This is the message which throbs through his book. It is also the message which throbs through his life and death. This encounter, he claimed, cannot be learned by reading about it but only through faith and experience. As his biographer recalls:

He told me often that everything he found in books, all that he wrote himself, seemed insipid compared with the grandeur of God and Jesus Christ, which faith would reveal to him. To quote him: "He alone is able to make himself known as he really is. We seek in reasoning and in the sciences, as in a bad copy, for what we neglect to see in an excellent original. God depicts himself in the depths of our soul, and we are not willing to see him there."[1]

Contemplate Christ

In other words, in addition to the other methods we have considered in this book already: pray 'on the hoof', set long-term goals, set short-term goals, pull into life's lay-bys and pace yourself, ever conscious that God is the axis of all our activity, Brother Lawrence stresses the importance of contemplating Christ himself.

Such contemplation brings the Christian to the still point where every part of their being is open to the love which always streams from the face of God to his children. Such contemplation makes absorption of the divine love not only possible but natural. Such contemplation gives rise to the desire, if necessary, to suffer for the Beloved. It is moving to read how Brother Lawrence reached this climax of love given and received. Three months before he died, he wrote in a letter to one of his disciples: 'Pains and suffering will be a Paradise for me, so be I shall suffer with God, and the greatest pleasures would be a Hell, if I tasted them without him. All my consolation would be to suffer something for him.'[2]

Contemplation not only gives rise to the willingness to suffer, it brings with it a deep-down heart-awareness that the One we love is indeed Immanuel, God with us. This assurance permeated Brother Lawrence's whole being. Just two weeks before he died, he reminded another of his followers: 'He is in our midst. Let us seek him nowhere else.'[3]

When we know with a through-and-through knowing that God is with us, our minds and hearts turn to him almost automatically, in the same way as the thoughts and love of lovers stay with one another all day and every day even when they are separated by

continents. So, in the months leading up to his death, he urges another of his correspondents to: 'Forget him as little as you can.'[4]

Writing to the same person two months later, he emphasises that being in love with God affects everything we do as well as who we are: 'We must prevent our mind wandering away, whatever be the occasion. We must make of our heart a temple of the

Spirit, where we may worship continually. We must set unbroken guard over ourselves, that we do nothing, think nothing, which could displease him.'5

He speaks with great passion when he spells out the prerequisites for practising the presence of God:

All [our] acts of worship must arise from faith, and the belief that in truth God is in our hearts ... We must worship him, love him and serve him in spirit and in truth. He sees all that which comes to pass, in us and in all his creatures. He exists apart from everything, and is the one on whom all other creatures depend. He is infinite in all perfection and merits by his boundless excellence and sovereign power all that we are.'6

Recognise your unworthiness

That is not to say that our ever-deepening relationship with God is laced with unmitigated joy. As in all human loving, a certain amount of pain is involved. The monk warns that whenever a person enjoys a heightened awareness of the presence of God, it is accompanied by a sense of unworthiness. In *The Spiritual Maxims* he puts it this way:

When we undertake the spiritual life, we must bear in mind who we are, and we shall realise that we are ... unworthy of the name of Christian, subject to all manner of tribulations ... which make us uneven in health, moods ... and of behaviour.7

Brother Lawrence was acutely aware of his own short-comings and innate sinfulness but, as we have observed, these did not cause him to grovel at the foot of Christ's cross with a constant beating of the breast or an unhealthy, introspective gazing of the navel. It drew from him ever-fresh songs of praise, awe and thanksgiving – songs not merely sung with his lips but enfleshed in a life of devoted love.

Teachers of prayer down the centuries have similarly endeavoured to engender within us the twin awareness of our own worthlessness and God's great goodness. This has been evident from the seventh century when St John Climacus spoke of the 'joy-creating sorrow' to the contemporary writer Ian Petit who puts the Gospel in a nutshell when he writes:

> The story of the Fall isn't just about how God's special creatures went wrong: it is about how those special creatures and all their descendents become damaged and bent, while remaining exceedingly gifted . . . We did not become sinners the day we committed our first sin. *We were born sinners.* We are sons and daughters of our fallen parents . . . We were conceived in sin . . . We come into existence as hostile to God. God was meant to be the centre of our being, the purpose of our existence. Because of sin [we have] become off-centre and we have taken the central place in our lives. Therefore God is viewed with suspicion. His very hands stretched out to save us are seen as hands reaching out to unseat us . . . We [even] see God as a rival. It is the Holy Spirit who convicts, that is, convinces us we are sinners – and he only does this in order to comfort us with the truth that there

is a remedy in Jesus Christ ... It is good to
know that Jesus Christ is the Saviour, but we
can rush to him begging to be saved from all sorts
of troubles and fail to ask to be saved from our sin
because we are not aware how sinful we are.[8]

Or, as Thomas Merton once expressed it:

Christianity is a religion for [people] who are
aware that there is a deep wound, a fissure
of sin that strikes down to the very heart of
[mankind's] being ... One reason why our
meditation never gets started is perhaps that
we never make this real, serious return to
the centre of our own nothingness before God.
Hence we never enter into the deepest reality
of our relationship with him.[9]

Brother Lawrence was ever-conscious of his nothingness before God. He would surely have applauded
the approach to prayer advocated by another contemporary writer who explains how to come to
God when we are oppressed by personal sin and
failure or overwhelmed by a general sense of our
own unworthiness:

Confess your sins and failings and beg God's forgiveness, thanking him for hearing your prayer.
    Then face him as you are: sinful, spiritually
handicapped and disabled in many ways; a
chronic patient. Accept these handicaps and
disabilities because he accepts you as you are
and loves you as you are.
    Refuse to nurse a sense of guilt. Instead,
embrace God's forgiveness and love ... His

goodness is greater than your badness. Accept his joy in loving and forgiving you.[10]

Feast on God's goodness

God's goodness is greater than our badness. This is the good news which Brother Lawrence relished. He would most certainly have echoed the much-loved General Thanksgiving which used to be part of the Church of England liturgy:

> We Thine unworthy servants
> do give Thee most humble and hearty thanks
> for all Thy goodness and loving kindness to us
> and to all [people].
> We bless Thee for our creation, preservation and
> all the blessings of this life.[11]

Right up to the moment of his death, the awareness of the goodness of God strengthened him every step of the way. In his maxims he encourages us similarly to feast on God's goodness so that we may confront our Achilles' heel:

> We should seek to learn the sins that do most easily beset us, and the times and occasions when we do most often fall. In the time of struggle we ought to have recourse to God with perfect confidence, abiding steadfast in the Presence of His Divine Majesty: in lowly adoration we should tell out before Him our griefs and our failures, asking Him lovingly for the Succour of His grace; and in our weakness we shall find in Him our strength.[12]

This teaching, too, runs like a thread through the teaching on prayer handed down through the centuries. Building on the wealth of this teaching, James Houston likens us to Alice in Wonderland and insists that it is vital that, like her, we should be prepared to tumble headlong into the seemingly bottomless pit of our own inner emptiness –

> [those] dark, unexplored caverns in our own heart which have been created by the weaknesses we are afraid to name or the childhood memories which we have repressed or ignored even though they have scarred and wounded us.
>
> We have to go down that hole because unless I know my basic need emotionally, temperamentally, spiritually, then I will always be struggling to do without God. But when you fall down that hole there is no one to support you. You just fall and fall until you discover that underneath are the everlasting arms.
>
> If we're ever to grow spiritually, we have to locate our Achilles' heel, where we limp. This is where we meet God. There God I need you profoundly.[13]

The God we need is the God who is able to heal and to change us. When this happens we shall be able to testify with Paul: 'Where I was weak, now I am strong.'

Thomas Merton underlines that it is part of the monastic tradition to encourage the monk to confront his own humanity in this way. He testifies to its value:

From the darkness comes light. From death, life. From the abyss there comes, unaccountably, the mysterious gift of the Spirit sent by God to make all things new, to transform the created and redeemed world and to re-establish all things in Christ.[14]

I was thinking about these challenges while I was reading on the beach one day. My husband and I had gone there early to swim and read and pray before the crowds arrived. Suddenly the tranquillity of the bay was turned into turbulence by the arrival of an extrovert American who stripped off everything but his bathing trunks, dived into the warm water and proceeded to shriek in excitement and glee from his pulpit in the sea.

Resentment rose in me reminding me of one of my own Achilles' heels: intolerance – particularly with seemingly insensitive extroverts! Instead of trying to ignore or repress my impatience and intolerance, I decided to take James Houston's advice seriously, to explore this inner abyss. I found myself falling, not into a bottomless pit, but into the arms of God who seemed to whisper: 'Be creative. Listen. Discover the good in the man.'

I listened as the man's shrill comments about the Mediterranean and the climate continued to echo around 'my' beach. But, in time, I noticed that he calmed down and I even forgot about him as the book I was reading absorbed my concentration. Suddenly, his voice burst into my consciousness again. This time it was gentle. When I looked up, I noticed him playing most sensitively with his children, wooing them into the warm water, teaching one to snorkel and encouraging the other to discover the delights of

the coloured stones which line the shore. I saw the good in him – the goodness of a father who loved his children enough to 'waste time' playing with them.

Nurture faith, hope and love

Feasting on God's goodness generates faith, hope and love, and Brother Lawrence emphasises that all three constitute food for the journey:

> He said that only faith, hope and love had to be nourished to become utterly dedicated to the will of God. All the rest was unimportant . . . All things are possible to him who believes, yet more to him who hopes, more still to him who

believes, yet more to him who practices and perseveres in these three virtues.[15]

By his 80th year, he had grown rich in faith. Faith is the ability to believe in the presence, commitment and love of the loved-one even when that person is separated from us by thousands of miles and we know we may never see them again. Over the years, the fear and guilt which tormented him when he first entered the monastery were replaced by unassailable faith:

> I see God by faith. And I see him in a way which could at times make me say, "I no longer believe, I see." I experience what faith teaches us and upon this assurance and practice of faith I shall live and die with him.[16]
> ... 'Faith enables me to touch him with my finger.'[17]

Such faith, he insists, germinates and grows in hearts which are aware of the presence of God in the middle of the maelstrom. Like blood being pumped around a person's body, it permeates every part of a Christian's life. Consequently, he pleaded with one sick friend to place their trust in their Creator: 'Put all your trust in him. You will soon see the results. We often delay healing by putting greater trust in remedies than in God.'[18]

To another, he wrote: 'God has many ways of drawing us to him, and sometimes conceals himself from us, but the simple faith which will not fail us in our time of need must be our support and the foundation of our trust which must be all in God.'[19]

And sixteen months before he died, he reiterated

the same message: 'I am well pleased with the trust you have in God. It is my wish that he increase it more and more. We shall not be able to have too much trust in a friend so good and faithful, who will never fail us in this world or the next.'[20]

Faith, according to the writer to the Hebrews, 'is being sure of what we hope for and certain of what we do not see'. (Heb 11:1) Brother Lawrence adds: 'We should put life into our faith',[21] recalling, no doubt, the further claim of the writer to the Hebrews: 'Without faith it is impossible to please God.' (Heb 11:6)

Hope

This means that, by faith, anyone from the commuter to the social worker, the young mum to the medics I mentioned at the beginning of this book, can see and hear and touch God in the 'muchness and manyness'[22] of their hectic lives. This is good news because faith kindles hope.

According to Brother Lawrence, hope is proportionate to our experienced intimacy with God. The more we feast, by faith, on the mystery and majesty, the tenderness and gentleness of God, the more our hope and expectations expand. Painting powerful pen-pictures, he offers this advice to one of his disciples: 'Hold yourself before God like a poor dumb person, or a paralytic at a rich man's gate . . . Keeping your mind in the presence of the Lord.'[23]

Just one month before he died, he exhorted one of his disciples to: 'Knock at the door, keep on knocking, and I say to you that in his own good time, he will open to you, if you are not discouraged, and . . .

he will suddenly give you what he has postponed for many years.'[24] Such hope engenders the grace of detachment: 'a scorn of earthly things'.

Hope does this by fanning the flames of our love for God into a blaze which consumes and turns to ashes all other desires and ambitions. They then lose their ability to attract or entice. To change the image, hope envisages God as the pearl of great price in comparison with whom all other treasures and all other loves: wealth, ambition, relationships, prestige, popularity and success all seem worthless. Such attachment to Christ and detachment from earthly ambition brings freedom. Brother Lawrence enjoyed the elixir of this freedom to the full. As his biographer recalls:

> One day I told him, without preparation, that something of great consequence which he had very close to his heart and for which he had worked a long time, could not be done, and that a resolution against the proposal had been adopted. To this he simply replied: "It must be accepted that those who thus decided have good reasons. It only remains to carry it out and say no more about it." This in fact he did so completely that, although he has since had frequent occasion to mention it, he has never said a word.[25]

Practising the presence of God had set him free from the snares of selfish ambition, selfish desires and selfish lusts: set him free to live, not for self, but wholly for Christ.

This veiled hint at conflict in the monastery contains a curiously contemporary ring and reveals the relevance of the practice of the presence of God for the business person, parents and Christians in leadership. Practising the presence of God gradually delivers us from our obsession with self and persuades us, instead, to place God at the centre of our universe.

Love

Love is the key. At least, that was Brother Lawrence's experience. He insisted that God cannot be known through the medium of the mind. He can only truly be known by love. Love gave him the strength gradually to emerge from a self-centred to a Christ-centred way of thinking:

> If the will can in any fashion understand God, it can only be through love . . .
>
> I do nothing else but abide in his holy presence, and I do this by a simple attentiveness and an habitual, loving turning of my eyes on him. This I should call . . . a wordless and secret conversation between the soul and God which no longer ends . . .[26]

Observations like these remind me of the father of a three-month-old child I watched on one occasion. Quite spontaneously, from time to time, this young man would pick up his baby, hold her in his huge hands and gaze at her curly eye-lashes and black, curly hair, her perfect finger-nails and smooth skin. As he gazed, he would smile with unashamed pride at this fruit of his love and clearly give his assent to the slogan on her T-shirt: God's precious gift.

It would appear that Brother Lawrence's relationship with God was more intimate even than the beautiful eye contact this father and baby so obviously enjoyed. Describing the ecstasy of love he experienced, like many other great men and women of prayer, he likened his relationship with God to a child and its mother; to a baby guzzling at God's breasts:

> My most usual method is this simple attention, loving, turning of my eyes to God, to whom I often find myself bound with more happiness and gratification than that which a baby enjoys clinging to its nurse's breast. So, if I dare use this expression, I should be glad to describe this condition as 'the breasts of God', for the inexpressible happiness I savour there.[27]

The picture language is powerful. When a baby is being breast-fed, it is totally absorbed in the comfort and nourishment which is flowing from the mother's body. It is caught up with the sense of union which is being stimulated and savoured. Such moments are healing moments when the child knows itself nurtured, nourished and 'known', in the fullest sense of that word; that is, deeply understood and intimately loved.

Such picture language is not unique to the monk. It is reminiscent of the language used by Isaiah and others:

> Can a mother forget the baby at her breast
>   and have no compassion on the child
>   she has borne?
> Though she may forget,

I will not forget you!
(Isaiah 49:15)

For you will nurse and be satisfied
   at her comforting breasts,
you will drink deeply
   and delight in her overflowing abundance.
(Isaiah 66:11)

On other occasions, the language he uses is that of lovers. Other teachers of prayer also frequently resort to this kind of terminology. As one contemporary writer puts it:

Do you remember when you first fell in love? Remember how you couldn't wait to be together – how long each moment was that you were apart? Remember how you felt when you heard that beloved voice, saw that beloved face?

Remember how you hung on every word – how you couldn't wait to talk every little thing over, how you never seemed to run out of things to share? Remember how much fun – how magical – everything was that you did together, no matter how ordinary and mundane? . . .

The originator of relationships – our Creator – wants a relationship with each one of us . . . We are offered all the excitement, joy and fulfilment of our first-love experience, all of the comfort of a good companion, and all the intimacy of someone who is vitally interested in every word and thought. He is always there. He never leaves us nor forsakes us. He's never too busy. He's always listening to us, and vitally interested in us. He is constantly available for intimate communion with us . . .

He made us to enjoy Him . . . We were made to seek the Lord as our intimate 'mate' – as the one whose presence we can't wait to bask in. We were made to share everything, every moment, every hope, every dream, every fear with Him. He truly is standing at the door of our hearts, knocking – and we are turning a deaf ear to that knocking. In doing so, we are missing out on our whole purpose for being. We are running around trying to "help God" and He is waiting to help us![28]

Brother Lawrence expresses the same sentiments with characteristic brevity: 'He is the father of the afflicted, always ready to help us. He loves us more than we think.'[29]

Two weeks before he died, while he was suffering considerable pain, we find rising from within him that same well-spring of confidence: 'If we knew how much he loves us, we should be ever ready to receive equally at his hand the sweet and the bitter. Even the most painful things and the most hard would be sweet and pleasing to us . . .'[30]

The intimacy he enjoyed with his Creator drew from him, in ever-increasing measure, a living response – the kind of embodiment of love Paul praises:

Love is patient, love is kind. It does not envy, it does not boast, it is not proud. It is not rude, it is not self-seeking, it is not easily angered, it keeps no record of wrongs. Love does not delight in evil but rejoices with the truth. It always protects, always trusts, always hopes, always perseveres. Love never fails. (1 Cor 13:4-8)

Love is patient. His biographer could write of Brother Lawrence: 'His patience had been great indeed through all his life, but . . . it waxed stronger than ever as he approached the end.'[31]

Love is kind. Similarly, the same biographer recalls the 'great kindness' with which the monk always greeted people.[32]

His life was so full of a joy which shone from his face and filled his lips and which he sometimes had difficulty restraining that there was no room for envy, keeping a record of wrongs, pride or boasting. Instead, thoughts of the Truth, Christ himself, filled his mind until his soul was flooded with unbroken peace. So much so that

> at last his faithfulness and patience won its rewards in the possession of his soul by a sense, unbroken and undisturbed, of the Presence of God. All his acts, in kind so varying and so multiplied in number, were changed into an unclouded vision, an illumined love, a joy uninterrupted.[33]

'All his acts.' Love flows from his letters as it must surely have streamed from his person to those he met: 'I am distressed to see you suffering so long,' he wrote to one of his correspondents shortly before his death even though he was in great personal pain himself.

In this, as in so many other characteristics, he resembles Jesus himself. I finished planning this chapter beside the Sea of Galilee on the beach I have mentioned before – where it is believed Jesus disembarked from the boat prior to feeding the five thousand. On that day, Jesus must have felt full of grief as he came to terms with the news he had just received: that his cousin, John the Baptist, had been beheaded by Herod. Yet when he saw the thousands who were flocking towards his landing-stage, love flowed from him. Instead of mourning the loss of his cousin, he healed and comforted the sick. True love always finds an outlet where its abundance may overflow.

Near that beach, God's love overflowed to me – not primarily from watching or joining the pilgrims at prayer, nor even through meditating or contemplating the compassionate Christ, but rather through visiting the holiday home for handicapped people hidden among the trees. There I met a nun peeling piles of potatoes for them. Something about the love and care with which she peeled away the skin *and* prised away the blemishes spoke to me of the love of Christ. There, too, I met some of the handicapped. The joy of the Risen Christ shone through their faces and, as one stretched out his hand to me in welcome, I felt through his unco-ordinated limbs the love of God.

Worship

Such expressions of love prompt praise and worship. To worship means, among other things, to demonstrate joy, to express love to God through intimacy, to come and adore, to rejoice in body, mind and spirit, to bow in reverence, to sing God's praises, to proclaim his worth-ship, to give thanks, to celebrate. Brother Lawrence urges us to do this:

We must, during all our labour and in all else

we do, even in our reading and writing . . . pause for some short moment, as often indeed as we can, to worship God in the depth of our heart, to savour him, though it be but in passing, and as it were by stealth. Since you are not unaware that God is present before you whatever you are doing, that he is at the depth and centre of your soul, why not pause from time to time at least from that which occupies you outwardly, even from your spoken prayers, to worship him inwardly, to praise him, petition him, to offer him your heart and thank him? What can God have that gives him greater satisfaction than that a thousand thousand times a day all his creatures should thus pause to withdraw and worship him in the heart.[34]

Such worship springs from faith – the belief:

that [God] sees all that which comes to pass, and that will come to pass, in us and in all his creatures; that he exists apart from everything, and is the one on whom all other creatures depend; that he is infinite in all perfection, and merits by his boundless excellence and sovereign power all that which we are, and all that which is in heaven and on earth, all of which he can dispose at his good pleasure in time and eternity.'[35]

Authentic worship is in spirit and in truth:

To worship God in truth is to recognise him for . . . what he is, that is to say infinitely perfect, infinitely to be adored, infinitely removed from evil and thus with every attribute divine . . . To worship God in truth is again to confess that . . . he greatly desires to make us like him if we will.[36]

To worship in spirit and in truth is to worship secretly: 'It is God alone who can see this worship, a worship we can so often repeat that in the end it becomes as if it were natural, and as if God were one with our soul and our soul one with God.'[37]

As David Adam explains, such worship was not foreign to the Celtic Church. It came naturally:

When we turn to the Celtic Church, we discover men and women who are quite simple, are not particularly clever or gifted, but to them, God is a living and glorious reality which supernaturalises their everyday life and transforms their most ordinary events into sublime worship. For them God is not of the past, or confined to the Bible or the Holy Land, but the Divine Reality to be encountered each day, in each event or each decision. This is a God of the now, involved in the present situation, and His will and way are to be discovered and followed. We arise today in the Divine Presence – and that is reality.[38]

Brother Lawrence might well have echoed this Celtic prayer:

The Father who created me
With eye benign beholdeth me;
The Son who dearly purchased me
With eye divine enfoldeth me;
The Spirit who so altered me
with eye refining holdeth me;

In friendliness and love the Three
Behold me when I bend the knee.[39]

On his death-bed, as throughout his life, he was
acutely aware of the presence of the God who loved
him. Here he displayed a fearlessness which amazed
his brother monks. The Abbot records:

> He was never in the least fretful, when he was
> most wracked with pain, joy was manifest not
> only on his countenance, but still more in his
> speech, so much so in fact that those who visited
> him were constrained to ask whether he was not
> suffering.[40]

'Yes, I do suffer,' Brother Lawrence replied, 'the
pains in my side sore trouble me, but my spirit is
happy and well content.'

> '"Suppose God will that you suffer for ten years,
> what then?" asked his brothers.
> '"I would suffer," the dying monk replied,
> "not for ten years only, but till the Day of
> Judgement, if it be God's will; and I would
> hope that He would continue to aid me with
> His grace to bear it joyfully."'[41]

Always aware that he was unworthy of God's love,
always anxious to suffer for the God who loved him
so faithfully and always longing to pay penance for
his many failures, he then begged his brothers to
turn him over onto his right side knowing that he
would feel intense pain. One of those watching him
die, twice offered to relieve this pain but each time
our hero replied: 'I thank you, my dear brother,

but I beg of you to let me bear just a little for the love of God.'[42]

It must have been moving for the brothers at the bedside to hear the dying man call out from time to time at the height of his suffering: 'My God, I worship Thee in my infirmities. Now, now, I shall have something to bear for Thee, – good, be it so, may I suffer and die with Thee.' To hear him recite part of the fifty-first Psalm: 'Create in me a clean heart, O God. Cast me not away from Thy Presence. Restore unto me the joy of Thy salvation.'[43]

Would they ever forget those moments when their brother cried out: 'Oh, Faith, Faith,' as he frequently did in the final hours of his life. Or, after he had received the last Sacrament, his response when one of his brothers asked him what occupied his mind: 'I am doing what I shall do, through all eternity – blessing God, praising God, adoring God, giving Him the love of my whole heart. It is our *one business*, my brethren, to worship Him and love Him, without thought of anything else.'

Would they not always cherish the memory of the manner of his death? In the words of the Abbot:

On Monday, the 12th of February 1691, at nine o'clock in the morning, without any pain or struggle, without losing in the slightest the use of any of his faculties, Brother Lawrence passed away in the embrace of his Lord, and rendered his soul to God in the peace and calm of one who had fallen on sleep.[44]

Paul once wrote:

The time has come for my departure. I have

fought the good fight, I have finished the race, I have kept the faith. Now there is in store for me the crown of righteousness, which the Lord, the righteous Judge, will award to me on that day – and not only to me, but also to all who have longed for his appearing. (2 Tim 4:7-8)

Brother Lawrence could have testified similarly. Instead, with characteristic humility and a deep desire that others should enjoy the unbroken and undisturbed fellowship with God which was his privileged experience, he wrote:

O Loving Kindness, so old and still so new, I have been too late of loving Thee . . . I cared too little to employ my early years for God. Consecrate all yours to His love. If I had only known Him sooner, if I had only had someone to tell me then what I am telling you, I should not have so long delayed in loving Him. Believe me, count as lost each day you have not used in loving God.[44]

For personal reflection

1. Get into the habit of tracing God's goodness expressed in your own life by setting aside a few minutes each day when you can watch an action replay of the past 24 hours. Home in on the good things God has given you during that period. Thank him for these good gifts.

2. Set aside a few minutes, each day if possible, to ask God to shine his torch on anything in your life which needs to be confessed. When it becomes clear what the failures are, make sure that, as well as confessing, you receive God's freely-offered forgiveness.

3. From time to time, be aware of *your* Achilles' heel. Explore the dark, hidden caverns of your own heart. Don't be afraid of the powerful emotions or inflexible attitudes you find there. Befriend them by offering them to God. Let them prompt you to pray that God will heal, transform and strengthen you so that every layer of your personality brings glory to him.

4. Ponder Brother Lawrence's claim: 'Faith enables me to touch [God] with my finger.' Think of occasions when you could echo that from your own experience.

5. Do what Brother Lawrence suggests: imagine that you have been denied the gift of speech and that you come into the presence of the God of Love. What happens? Or imagine that you are paralysed and that you lie at the gate of a rich man: God himself. What happens? Talk to God about your findings.

6. Think about the picture language Brother Lawrence used to describe his relationship with God: the baby at God's breasts, the lover and the Beloved. What kind of reactions do these produce in you? How would you describe your own love for God?

7. What place does spontaneous worship play in your own life? What might that be saying about your love for God?

8. Think about and respond to this claim:

   wordswithoutspacemakenosense
   wordswithout space makenosense
   words without space make no sense

   lifewithoutspacemakesnosense
   lifewithout space makesnosense
   life without space makes no sense

   make space for God
   even in the fast lane.[46]

9. Ask yourself: Why am I so busy? Is it a neurosis? Am I trapped into busyness? Is it an escape? Or is it creative, fulfilling, an expression of the abundant, joy-filled life given by God? Talk to God about your discovery.

10. Reflect on Brother Lawrence's claim:
    'You will find great delight and consolation when you apply your mind carefully, even in the midst of your business, to the presence of God. Always considers Him as *with* you as well as *in* you.'[47]

NOTES

Introduction

1. *The Practice of the Presence of God*, Mowbrays, London, 1980 p.iii-iv
2. E.M. Blaiklock (Trans), *The Practice of the Presence of God*, Hodder & Stoughton, London, 1989 p.56
3. E.M.Blaiklock (Trans), *The Practice of the Presence of God*, Hodder and Stoughton, London, 1989
4. Louis Gifford Parkhurst Jr., *The Believer's Secret of the Abiding Presence*, Word Publishing (UK), 1989
5. Robert Llewellyn, *An Oratory of the Heart: Daily Readings with Brother Lawrence*, DLT, London, 1984
6. Gael O'Leary RSM. Unpublished meditation
7. Throughout this book I have used the pronoun 'he' when mentioning God. This is my custom but I am aware that some readers may find this a stumbling block. I would like, therefore, to underline that, although I normally call God Lord or Father, my concept of God is much broader than those words would suggest. I believe the Bible encourages us to think, not only of the fatherly qualities of God but of the motherly qualities also – to worship and be nourished by a God who is tender as well as strong, gentle as well as wise, sensitive as well as omnipotent. I sense that breadth of understanding of God peeping through the pages of *The Practice of the Presence of God* also.

Chapter 1

1. A Week of Guided Prayer is a retreat which takes place 'in the stream of life'. The person attending the retreat attempts to carve out up to half an hour a day for prayer and meditation. They then meet with a prayer guide for up to half an hour a day to discuss the fruit of their meditation.
2. E.M. Blaiklock op.cit. p.46
3. Mowbrays op.cit. p.2
4. E.M. Blaiklock op.cit. p.19
5. The Cistercians in New Zealand, Fr. Conleth OCSO *Sing No Sad Songs for Me*, compiled by Sister Mary Damian RSM, A H and A W Read, 1971
6. Ibid. No page.
7. Mowbrays op.cit. p.23
8. Philippians 4:13 Jerusalem Bible
9. Mowbrays, op.cit. p.23
10. *The Character of Brother Lawrence*, Pub:H.R. Allenson p.47 (No date, no editor)
11. Ibid. p.48
12. Mowbrays, op.cit. p.42
13. Mowbrays, op.cit. p.43
14. David Adam, *The Cry of the Deer* SPCK Triangle 1993 p.105
15. E.M. Blaiklock op.cit. p.29
16. *Gathered Thoughts of Brother Lawrence*, Pub: H.R. Allenson, p.59
17. Sir John Ford KCMG. MC, Unpublished meditations on *The Practice of the Presence of God*

Chapter 2

1. E.M.Blaiklock op.cit.p.73
2. Ibid. p.73
3. Ibid. p.73
4. Mowbrays, op,cit. p.32
5. Ibid. p.47

6. Ibid. p.47
7. Ibid. p.52
8. David Adam, *Power Lines*, SPCK Triangle, London 1992 p.x
9. Douglas Steere, *Introduction to A Testament of Devotion*, Thomas Kelly, The Upper Room, 1955, p.10
10. Mark Virkler *Dialogue With God*, Bridge Publishing, 1986 p.29
11. Sue Monk Kidd, *God's Joyful Surprise* Hodder and Stoughton, 1990 p.120–121
12. See David Adam, *The Eye of the Eagle*, *Edges of His Glory*, *Tides and Seasons* and *Power Lines*, SPCK Triangle, 1989 p.20
13. David Adam, *Tides and Seasons*, SPCK Triangle, 1989 p.20
14. Brother Ramon, *Heaven on Earth*, Marshall Picking 1991 p.27
15. David Adam, *Power Lines*, op. cit. p.xii
16. Mowbrays, op. cit. p.32
17. Source not found.
18. E.M. Blaiklock op.cit. p.30
19. Ibid. p.22
20. Louis Gifford Parkhurst Jr., *The Believer's Secret of the Abiding Presence*, Word (UK) Ltd 1989, p.57
21. E.M. Blaiklock, op.cit. p.67
22. Louis Parkhurst (Trans), *The Believer's Secret of the Abiding Presence*, Word (UK) Ltd, 1989, p.120
23. *The Character*, op.cit. p.41
24. *Gathered Thoughts of Brother Lawrence*, Pub. H.R. Allenson Ltd, op.cit. p.54
25. *The Character of Brother Lawrence*, Pub. H.R. Allenson p.36
26. E.M. Blaiklock, op cit. p.22
27. Ibid, p.23
28. Ibid, p.85
29. Mowbrays op.cit. p.25
30. Mowbrays op.cit. p.25
31. *The Character of Brother Lawrence*, op.cit. p.39

32. Joy Davidman, Quoted Sue Monk Kidd, *God's Joyful Surprise*, op.cit.
33. Source Unknown
34. Blaiklock op.cit. p.75
35. Louis Gifford Parkhurst, Jr., *The Believer's Secret of the Abiding Presence*, Word (UK) Ltd., 1989, p.17
36. E.M. Blaiklock op.cit. p.22
37. Ibid. p.39–40
38. Ibid. p.49
39. Ibid. p.37
40. Ibid. p.36
41. David Adam, *Border Lands*, SPCK, London, 1991, p.16

Chapter 3

1. *The Spiritual Maxims*, op.cit. p.23
2. E.M. Blaiklock, op.cit. p.43
3. Louis Gifford Parkhurst Jr., op.cit. p.25
4. Mowbrays op.cot. p.21–22
5. David Goodall, *The Tablet*, Lent, 1992
6. Sue Monk Kidd op.cit. p.28
7. Joyce Huggett, *Prayer Journal*, Marshall Pickering
8. Louis Parkhurst Gifford Jr., op.cit. p.25
9. Jackie Pullinger, *Crack in the Wall*, Hodder and Stoughton 1989 p.28
10. Charles Wesley 1708–88
11. Kallistos Ware, *The Power of the Name*, Fairacres Publication, 43 1980 p.6
(This is an excellent introduction to the Jesus Prayer for those who would like to learn more about this way of praying.)
12. Paul Wallis, *Rough Ways in Prayer*, SPCK Triangle, 1991 p.82
13. Ibid. p.81
14. Ibid. p.81
15. E.M. Blaiklock op.cit. p.23
16. Louis Parkhurst Gifford Jr. op.cit. p.25
17. Ibid. p.25

Chapter 4

1. *The Spiritual Maxims*, op.cit. p.15
2. Catherine de Hueck Doherty, *Poustinia*, Fount 1975, p.20
3. Ibid. p.21
4. Ibid. p.22
5. Ibid. p.21
6. Sue Monk Kidd, *God's Joyful Surprise*, Hodder and Stoughton p.133
7. Teildhard de Chardin, *Le Milieu Divin*, Collins, 1975, pp.36-37
8. E.M. Blaiklock op.cit. p.41
9. *The Character of Brother Lawrence*, op.cit. p.48–49
10. Catherine de Hueck Doherty, op.cit. p.91
11. E.M. Blaiklock, op.cit. p.68–69
12. George Herbert 1593–1633
13. Sue Monk Kidd op.cit.
14. *The Character of Brother Lawrence*, op.cit. p.34
15. Anonymous
16. James E. Magaw quoted in *Alive Now*! July/August 1989, p.24

Chapter 5

1. Thomas Merton, *Contemplative Prayer*, DLT, 1983 p.31
2. Office of Compline
3. Thomas Merton. Quoted Esther de Waal, *A Seven Day Journey With Thomas Merton*, Eagle, 1992 p.40
4. Ibid. p.41
5. Sue Monk Kidd, *God's Joyful Surprise*, Hodder and Stoughton, 1987
6. Ibid. p.49
7. Sue Monk Kidd ibid. p.61
8. The image of prayer as a giant cartwheel was used by Laurence Freeman in an article in *The Tablet* on the 21st march 1992. I found it helpful and have developed it here.

9. St Augustine's description of the Bible

10. and 11. The magazine *Vision* published by the National Retreat Association and the book *Away From It All*, give details of many places where people can go to be still for a Quiet Day or for a residential retreat.

12. John Woolley, *I Am With You*, Crown, 1991 p.76

13. Brother Lawrence, *The Spiritual Maxims*, Pub. H.R. Allenson op.cit. p.14

14. Michael Green, *I Believe in Satan's Downfall*, Hodder and Stoughton, 1984 p.53

15. Ibid. p.72–73

16. Ibid. p.48

17. Fr. Matta al. Meskeen, quoted *Turning Over a New Leaf: Protestant Missions and the Orthodox Churches of the Middle East*, p.95

18. E.M. Blaiklock, op.cit. p.58

19. Ibid. p.48

20. Ibid. p.53

Chapter 6

1. E.M. Blaiklock op.cit. p.82

2. Ibid. p.55

3. Ibid. p.62

4. Ibid. p.58

5. Ibid. p.61

6. Ibid. p.70

7. Ibid. p.67

8. Ian Petit OSB, *The God Who Speaks*, DLT, 1989 p.23

9. Thomas Merton, *Contemplative Prayer*, DLT, 1983 p.134 and 86

10. Jim Borst, *Coming to God*, Eagle, 1992 p.34

11. Book of Common Prayer, The General Thanksgiving

12. *The Spiritual Maxims*, Pub. H.R. Allenson op.cit. p.17

13. James Houston, *Discipleship of Devotion*, Taped talk given at the London Institute for Contemporary Christianity

14. Thomas Merton op.cit. p.28
15. E.M. Blaiklock op.cit. p.30
16. Ibid. p.55
17. Ibid. p.59
18. Ibid. p.54
19. Ibid. p.58
20. Ibid. p.52
21. Ibid. p.20
22. Richard Foster's phrase
23. E.M. Blaiklock, op.cit. p.49
24. Ibid. p.61
25. Ibid. p.87
26. Ibid. p.73
27. Mowbrays, op.cit. p.32
28. Jan Ord, 'I Stand at the Door', article published in *Union Life*, Jan/Feb. 1993
29. Ibid. p.60
30. Ibid. p.62
31. Ibid. p.91
32. Ibid. p.82
33. Ibid. p.84
34. Ibid. p.69
35. Ibid. p.70
36. Ibid. p.71
37. Ibid. p.71
38. David Adam, *The Cry of the Deer*, SPCK Triangle, 1993 p.98
39. Ibid. p.105
40. *The Character of Brother Lawrence*, H.M. Allenson, op.cit. p.42
41. Ibid. p.43
42. Ibid. p.43
43. Ibid. p.43
44. Ibid. p.44
45. Ibid. p.60
46. My adaptation of George White's meditation published in *Alive Now!*. July/August 1989
47. Louis Gifford Parkhurst Jr., op.cit. p.69

The Exploring Prayer Series
Edited by Joyce Huggett

Exploring Prayer has the ambition to encourage and build
up private worship. Each book uses the author's hard-won
experience to point the reader to God – the One who listens
and answers. Authors have been encouraged to draw upon
their own Church tradition so that all can benefit from
the riches of the various strands of the Church: catholic,
evangelical and charismatic. The photographs in each book
have been chosen to reinforce the text.

Angela Ashwin
PATTERNS NOT PADLOCKS
Prayer for parents and all busy people, suggesting practical
ideas and initiatives for prayer building on the chaotic,
busy-ness of everyday life.

James Borst
COMING TO GOD
A stage by stage introduction to a variety of ways of using
times of stillness, quiet and contemplative meditation.

Michael Mitton
THE SOUNDS OF GOD
Helpful hints on hearing the voice of God, drawn from the
contemplative, evangelical and charismatic traditions.

Gerald O'Mahony
FINDING THE STILL POINT
Writing from his own experience of severe mood
swings, the author provides a means to understand erratic
moods and feelings so as to find the 'still' point, a safe
haven.

Heather Ward
STREAMS IN DRY LAND
Praying when God is distant, when you feel bored or
frustrated with your prayer life – or even empty, arid and
deserted by God.